1866-1991

125th

ANNIVERSARY

KITCHEN FUN FOR KIDS

Also by Michael Jacobson

The Complete Eater's Digest and Nutrition Scoreboard

Food for People, Not for Profit
(with Catherine Lerza)

The Fast Food Guide
(with Sarah Fritschner)

Salt: The Brand Name Guide to Sodium Content
(with Bonnie F. Liebman and Greg Moyer)

Safe Food
(with Lisa Y. Lefferts and Anne Garland)

Also by Laura Hill

Eating the Low-Fat Way

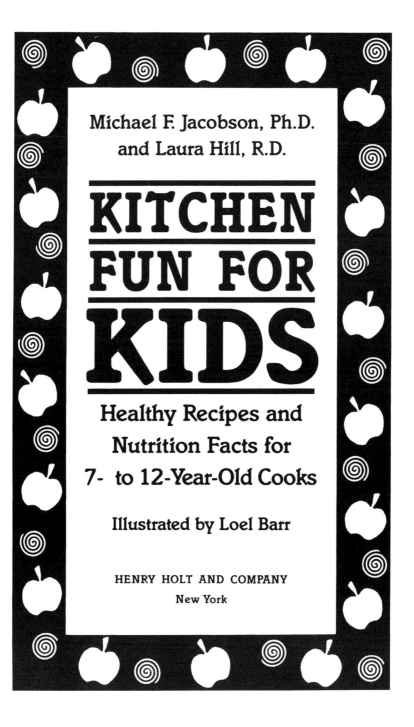

Michael F. Jacobson, Ph.D.
and Laura Hill, R.D.

KITCHEN
FUN FOR
KIDS

Healthy Recipes and
Nutrition Facts for
7- to 12-Year-Old Cooks

Illustrated by Loel Barr

HENRY HOLT AND COMPANY
New York

Published by Henry Holt and Company, Inc.,
115 West 18th Street, New York, New York 10011.
Published in Canada by Fitzhenry & Whiteside Limited,
195 Allstate Parkway, Markham, Ontario L3R 4T8.

Library of Congress Cataloging-in-Publication Data
Jacobson, Michael F.
Kitchen fun for kids : healthy recipes and nutrition facts for
7- to 12-year-old cooks / Michael Jacobson and Laura Hill; illustrated
by Loel Barr.—1st ed.
p. cm.
Includes index.
Summary: Recipes for sixty nutritional meals, including breakfast,
lunch, and supper. Each recipe presents one or two nutritional facts
through the illustrations.
ISBN 0-8050-1609-0
1. Cookery—Juvenile literature.   2. Nutrition—Juvenile
literature.   [1. Cookery.   2. Nutrition.]   I. Hill, Laura.
II. Barr, Loel, ill.   III. Title.
TX652.5.J34   1991
641.5—dc20   90-21370
CIP
AC

Henry Holt books are available at special discounts
for bulk purchases for sales promotions, premiums,
fund-raising, or educational use. Special editions
or book excerpts can also be created to specification.
For details contact:
Special Sales Director, Henry Holt and Company, Inc.,
115 West 18th Street, New York, New York 10011.

First Edition

Designed by Katy Riegel

Manufactured in Canada by Webcom Limited
Recognizing the importance of preserving the written word,
Henry Holt and Company, Inc., by policy, prints all of its
first editions on acid-free paper. ∞
1   3   5   7   9   10   8   6   4   2

ACKNOWLEDGMENTS

We thank Margaret and Julia Bensfield (now 10 and 7 years old) for inspiring the idea for this cookbook, Angela Cox for helping us figure out the book's ingredients, and Richard Layman for persuading us to actually cook it up.

We also thank Patricia Moshos and her enthusiastic third grade class at the Oakmont Elementary School in Havertown, Pennsylvania, and all the teachers, parents, and children who assisted in developing, testing, and tasting the recipes.

CONTENTS

PREFACE FOR PARENTS

Too many kids learn about food from television. Ad after ad extols the latest sugary breakfast cereal or the newest toy that McDonald's offers with its Happy Meals. The ads suggest to kids that if they eat a certain candy bar or drink a certain soft drink, they'll have lots of fun and friends. Your kids will rarely see ads or public-service messages pushing fresh fruit salad or carrot sticks or cooking at home.

Taking your kids with you to the supermarket means having them tempted by cartoon characters on frozen, microwavable meals, junky cereals placed at child's eye level, and candy displays at the checkout counter.

Is it any surprise that the Microwave Generation of kids is fatter than any previous generation . . . has little understanding of how what they eat affects their health . . . and doesn't have the foggiest idea how to use a stove or a cookbook? Is it any surprise that American children have higher cholesterol levels and blood pressures than children in nations whose diets are lower in fat, cholesterol, and sodium?

Kitchen Fun for Kids is designed to introduce kids not only to the kitchen but also to healthy eating. The recipes are appropriate for kids 7 to 12 years of age. The level of difficulty—"Rookie," "Intermediate," "Master"—is given for each recipe.

The recipes provide optimal nutrition, child-pleasing taste, and convenience. The ingredients used are wholesome, and very few recipes use sugar, white flour, or egg yolks.

All of the dishes—even the desserts—are far healthier than typical supermarket fare or recipes in most other cookbooks for children (or adults, for that matter).

The recipes and nutritional facts are easily understood by kids. But you'll probably have to explain the nutritional analyses that accompany each recipe. According to groups such as the National Academy of Sciences and the American Heart Association, a recommended daily diet for 7- to 10-year-old boys and girls should provide about 2,000 calories and up to 70 grams (15 teaspoons) of fat, 2,000 milligrams of sodium (that is equivalent to 5,000 milligrams, or 1 teaspoonful, of salt), and 200 milligrams of cholesterol. Good diets for 11- and 12-year-olds would contain 10 percent (for girls) to 20 percent (for boys) more calories, fat, sodium, and cholesterol. It's virtually impossible to construct diets that are healthy from processed foods or fast foods. The recipes in this book, however, call for fresh, minimally processed, and low-salt and low-fat foods, and will enable your children to cook up a great diet.

You and your children should also read together the Golden Safety Rules (page 1), which touch on kitchen safety and basic cooking techniques. What with sharp knives and hot stoves, kitchens can be dangerous places. A little care will make them safe.

Many of the recipes require the use of a gas or electric stove or oven. We don't rely on microwave ovens because we think it is important for children to learn how to use traditional kitchen appliances.

Teaching your children to cook at a young age will endow

them with a basic skill, and a pleasure, that will last a lifetime. Cooking provides kids with an opportunity for creativity, an avenue to self-reliance, a means of obtaining taste sensations missing from restaurant and store-bought food, and insights into the natural world from which food comes. Cooking introduces and accustoms your kids to the tastes and textures of real foods, including many foods never included in prepared meals.

For you, the time spent cooking with your children is enriching, rewarding, and useful quality time. But, needless to say, it will require care and patience. Kids (like many adults) can be slow and messy. You'll need to have the right foods on hand. And you'll need to be calm and encouraging, even when milk is spilling off the countertop. Complications notwithstanding, teaching your kids to cook can be lots of fun.

We hope that you and your children enjoy using *Kitchen Fun for Kids* as much as we've enjoyed writing it for you.

INTRODUCTION
Food Is More Important Than You Think

A big, crisp, red apple after school. A giant plate of spaghetti and tomato sauce when you're starving. A juicy orange or crunchy carrot for lunch.

Eating can be fun and delicious. Some people like to eat at a restaurant or stick a frozen dinner in a microwave oven. But what we like best is to cook our own meals at home.

There is nothing more exciting than going out to our garden and picking a fresh, ripe, huge, red, delicious tomato. We sometimes slice it up for a salad or sandwich. Or we dice it into tiny pieces and use it in a spaghetti sauce.

But when we don't have homegrown foods—and that's most of the time—we like to open a cookbook and find a mouth-watering new recipe. We collect the ingredients from the refrigerator and kitchen shelves, prepare them according to the recipe's directions, and then cook them up. Our families and friends usually love the food, and we feel great.

Kitchen Fun for Kids tells you how to prepare dozens of tasty dishes. There are recipes for your tongue's every mood: cold, refreshing drinks; tangy fruit salads; delicious, easy-to-make main courses; and soups that you will love.

Some of the recipes are so easy that even beginning chefs will look like experts. If you have not cooked much, you may want to start with the simpler recipes ranked "Rookie." As you become more experienced, move on to the harder ones graded "Intermediate" and "Master." (Don't worry, none of the recipes is very hard.)

WHY FOOD IS SO IMPORTANT

Some people think the only purpose of eating is for taste. If something tastes good, your tongue tells your brain, "Wow! Give me another bite."

Your tongue cares about only one thing: taste. But the rest of your body needs more than sweet, salty, or crispy foods. Your body needs healthy, nutritious foods to help it grow as strong and smart as it can. Everything you are made of—skin, hair, muscles, feet, brain, ears, blood, and fingernails—is made from the food you eat. It had better be good!

Without enough of the right kinds of foods, you won't be as healthy as you could be. And too many of the wrong kinds of food can actually make you sick.

Your body needs about forty different substances to build muscles, bones, skin, and all the other parts of your body. It must get all of those substances, called *nutrients, from food.*

Foods provide:

- *Carbohydrates*: The energy source in our foods. There are three types of carbohydrates: starch, sugar, and fiber.
  Starch: Potatoes, bread, and spaghetti are mostly starch. Your body uses starch for energy to help you play, run, think, and wash the dishes.
  Sugar: That's what makes honey, raisins, apples, and candy bars taste sweet. After your tongue is tickled pink by sugar, your body uses the sugar for energy.

Fiber: Vegetables, fruit, beans, and other foods made from plants contain fiber. It is in potato skins, apple peels, oranges, and whole-wheat bread. It is never found in hamburgers, hot dogs, ice cream, cheese, or other foods that come from animals. Unlike vitamins, minerals, and protein, fiber is valuable because the body *cannot* digest it. More about this a little later.

- *Protein*: Eggs, fish, chicken, meat, milk, cheese, and beans are rich in protein. Your body turns the proteins in food into muscles, hair, and other things. Almost everyone eats plenty of protein (maybe even too much).

- *Fat*: That's what makes margarine, butter, and fatty meat so greasy. Vegetable oil is pure fat. Some of the fat that we eat—margarine, for example—is easy to see. But other fat is hidden in peanut butter, hot dogs, whole milk, candy bars, buttered popcorn, hamburgers, and American cheese. Your body needs some fat, but most people eat far too much fat. A child between 7 and 12 years old should not eat more than about 15 teaspoons of fat a day. If you were to eat a Double Whopper and a big of fries at Burger King, you would use up your whole 15 teaspoons of fat in one meal!

- *Minerals*: Iron, calcium, zinc, and other minerals are found in rocks and also in natural foods. Some foods contain lots of one or two minerals, while other foods contain small amounts of many minerals. Calcium and phosphorus are minerals that help build bones and teeth. Iron is the mineral that makes blood red. Minerals also help the body turn food into energy, help muscles move, and enable our body to do everything else it does.

- *Vitamins*: To stay healthy, your body also needs vitamins. Vitamins are often called by letters and numbers, such as vitamin A, vitamin C, and vitamin B-1. You need vitamins from food because your body cannot make them itself. Vitamins help the body digest food, change food into energy, and do all of its other functions—like see, smell, feel, think, and chew—that people and animals do. Some foods have lots of vitamins, while others have very few vitamins. We should eat lots of different foods to get enough of all the different vitamins that our body needs.

GOOD GUYS AND BAD GUYS

A healthy diet gives you plenty of the good nutrients (like vitamins and minerals) and not too much fat, sugar, and other bad stuff. But if you eat too many candy bars, french fries, potato chips, hamburgers, hot dogs, and soft drinks, you won't get enough of the right nutrients, and you'll get too much sugar, fat, cholesterol, and sodium.

Sugar provides energy, but none of the nutrients that your body needs to build muscles or to work smoothly. As you know, bacteria—germs so small that they can only be seen through a microscope—in your mouth love sugar as much as you do. The bacteria turn sugar into acid, which eats into your teeth, making cavities. The recipes in this book use either no sugar or only a small amount of it. We want you to have healthy, cavity-free teeth.

The single worst part of most kids' and adults' diets is that they have too much *fat*. Fat contains twice as many calories as protein, sugar, or starch. Calories are a measure of energy that a food provides. People who exercise a lot need lots of energy—and calories. But most kids don't get nearly as much exercise as they should. Kids often are driven to school, instead of walking or biking. If you don't burn up the calories that fat gives you, *you* can get fat. More American children are fat now than ever before.

Foods that come from animals usually contain a kind of

fat—called saturated fat—that is bad for another reason. Slowly, over the years, the fat in meat, milk, and cheese causes slow changes in your arteries. Arteries are the small tubes that carry blood from your heart to your lungs to every part of your body.

The fat in meat and milk can lead to a waxy buildup in the arteries and make it harder and harder for the blood to pass

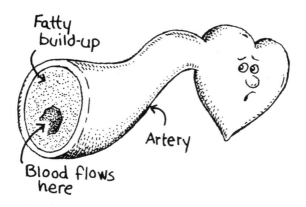

through. The closing of arteries takes many years, but it starts in childhood. If the opening in an artery gets too small, blood cannot pass through—just like a drinking straw that gets clogged in a thick shake. If an artery is too clogged to feed blood to the heart, the person will suffer a heart attack. If the artery cannot deliver blood to the brain, the person will suffer a stroke. Children almost never have heart attacks and strokes. But more American adults die of heart attacks than any other cause. Ask a parent if any of your adult relatives have had a heart attack.

Cholesterol is also greasy. You can't see it, but it is in meat, chicken, milk, cheese, and especially egg yolks. Cholesterol, too, slowly clogs arteries as people get older. That's why many of the recipes in *Kitchen Fun for Kids* call for only the whites of eggs, not the yolks. One egg yolk contains almost as much cholesterol as you should eat in a day. It is okay to eat whole eggs sometimes. Just don't eat them too often.

Fiber is something that most people don't get enough of. Fiber helps keep your large intestine cleaned out. The large intestine is the bottom part of the long tube that runs from your tummy to your tush. As food moves through the tube, nutrients and water in the food go through the walls of the tube and into your bloodstream. But fiber doesn't, and it helps move waste along. Many scientists believe that eating a life-long diet high in fiber keeps your intestines healthy, prevents constipation, and reduces the chances of getting cancer in adulthood.

One bonus of eating foods high in fiber is that they are usually delicious and contain little or no fat. Foods like cantaloupe, peaches, blueberries, grapes, celery, and carrots have lots of fiber; as you have probably guessed, so do most of our recipes.

Many of the recipes use whole-wheat flour instead of white flour. Both whole-wheat and white flour are made from wheat kernels. But many of the vitamins, minerals, and fiber that are naturally present in the wheat germ and wheat bran

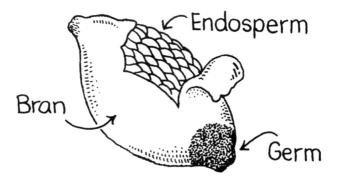

Wheat Kernel

are discarded when wheat kernels are ground into white flour. White flour consists primarily of the kernel's endosperm, which is low in vitamins and minerals. Some of the vitamins and minerals are added back to "enriched" white flour, but it still is not as good as whole-wheat flour. Whole-wheat flour contains all the nutrition of the wheat kernel.

Then there's salt. Our bodies don't need any more salt than that present in natural foods. But most packaged foods and restaurant foods are loaded with salt. Some people use their salt shaker to add lots of extra salt to their foods. A typical meal at Kentucky Fried Chicken gives you all the salt you should eat in an entire day (about 5,000 milligrams, or 1 teaspoonful).

The problem with salt is that eating too much of it for years can cause high blood pressure. That means that the blood presses too hard against a person's arteries, like too much pressure in a garden hose. The high pressure can injure the artery. Having high blood pressure for many years can cause a heart attack or a stroke.

"Salty" is the main flavor of many packaged foods, such as canned soup. Our recipes use plenty of real ingredients that have their own rich flavor. We did not need to add any salt at all to most of the recipes.

Finally, many packaged foods contain artificial colorings, artificial flavorings, preservatives, softeners, thickeners, and other additives. Some of the additives are useful. Preservatives can prevent bacteria from growing, and vitamins add to a food's nutritional value. But some additives—artificial colorings and flavorings—replace fruit and other nutritious ingredients. Caffeine, an additive in Coca-Cola and many other soft drinks, is the same stimulant that is present in coffee. A stimulant can make you "hyper" and make it hard for you to sleep. Some additives may cause allergic reactions or other health problems. One advantage of cooking your own foods from scratch is that you can avoid all of these additives.

With all these good guys and bad guys in food, eating a healthy diet may seem hard to do. Here are some tricks to help you:

- Eat less fat—that is the best eating change you can make
- Eat lots of fresh fruits and vegetables
- Eat whole-wheat bread instead of white bread
- Eat fewer hamburgers, hot dogs, fried chicken, french fries, and chips
- Eat low-fat dairy products, such as milk, yogurt, and cheese
- Eat less candy and cakes, and drink less soda pop
- Eat less butter, margarine, and mayonnaise

To help you (and your parents) understand how healthy the recipes in this book are, we list how many calories and how much fat, sodium, and cholesterol each recipe contains. As you now know, those are some of the bad guys to watch out for. All the recipes provide many of the good guys—protein, starch, fiber, vitamins, and minerals—that your body needs. These recipes call for skim or low-fat milk and yogurt because most of their fat has been removed.

SECRETS OF GREAT COOKS

The first time you use a recipe, be sure to follow the directions exactly. The second time, you may want to make changes that you think will make it taste better. Try adding blueberries or raisins if you want extra sweetness. Or add a spice or herb that you like the smell or taste of, such as cinnamon, nutmeg, or basil. Or use a little more whole-wheat flour and a little less white flour. Cooks are always changing recipes. That's part of the fun of cooking.

Another secret is that great cooks like to try new recipes with new ingredients. It's boring to make and eat hamburgers, spaghetti, and cheese sandwiches every day. Every time we go shopping, we try to buy at least one new vegetable, fruit, or other food. That way, we are always trying new foods and new recipes, and giving our tastebuds new treats.

Well, enough reading. It's cooking time, so pick a tempting recipe and get cookin'.

We hope you have fun in the kitchen!

BEFORE YOU BEGIN

Cooking is fun—almost as much fun as eating. To have the most fun in the kitchen, you should know the safety rules for chefs. You should also know how to use the appliances and tools in the kitchen.

THE GOLDEN SAFETY RULES

Safety is the most important cooking skill. Follow these safety rules whenever you are cooking.

1. *Always* use pot holders or oven mitts when you are putting things into or taking things out of the oven. Also wear your oven mitts when you are lifting lids from pots on the stove or removing pots and pans from the stove.
2. Keep your fingers out of the bowl when you are using an electric mixer. Never put your fingers or utensils into the blender while it is running. Be very careful when you are removing and cleaning the blade.
3. Ask an adult to teach you how to operate the stove,

broiler, and toaster oven. Don't touch the toaster or toaster oven when it is on. Always turn off the stove, oven, or other appliances as soon as you are finished using them.

4. Be careful when you use knives. Always use the handle of the knife—*never* touch the blade, especially the sharp side of the blade. Always chop food on a cutting board—never, never chop or slice food while you are holding it in your hand.

5. Never plug in appliances with wet hands.

6. Turn the handles of pots and pans on the stove toward the wall so that you don't accidentally knock over something hot. Hold the handle of pots and pans (with oven mitts on!) when you are stirring ingredients, so the pan doesn't slip off the burner.

7. Roll up your sleeves so they don't get caught on pot handles, get too close to the hot burner, or get dunked into ingredients. Wear an apron when you are cooking to protect your clothes.

8. Be very careful when you are opening cans because the lids are very sharp. Use a butter knife to lift up the lid, then grasp the lid in the center to throw it away. Never touch the rough, sharp edge.

9. If something you are cooking in a pot or pan catches on fire, cover the pot or pan with a tight-fitting lid to smother the fire, or dump baking soda onto the flames. Never use water to put out a fire in or near an electrical appliance. If something in the oven or toaster oven catches on fire, close the oven door and turn the oven off (if it is a toaster oven, unplug it). The fire will go out.

10. Wash your hands before you start to cook, and *always* wash your hands and cooking tools with hot, soapy water after handling raw chicken. A disease-causing bacterium called *salmonella* may be living

on the chicken. In properly cooked chicken, the heat of cooking kills *salmonella* bacteria.

WHAT'S WHAT: A SHORT INTRODUCTION TO THE KITCHEN

If you are not an experienced cook, ask an adult to give you a tour of the kitchen. Have him or her explain how to use the tools and appliances. For the first few times you cook, ask an adult to be your partner. Do not cook by yourself until your parents or your adult partner agrees that you are ready to do so.

To make cooking *so-o-o-o* much easier, read through the recipe completely from top to bottom. Collect all of the ingredients and tools that you will need before you begin. Arrange your tools on the work area so that you know exactly where everything is when you need it. When you are using the oven, adjust the oven rack so that it is positioned directly in the middle *before* you turn on the oven.

Finally, remember that the cook is responsible for leaving the kitchen clean and neat. To make the job a little easier, try to put things away as you use them, and fill dirty bowls, pots, and pans with water until you get around to washing them. It will make cleanup time a lot quicker.

HOW TO:

Crack an Egg

To crack an egg, hold it in your writing hand and tap the middle of the egg against the side of the bowl. Don't tap it too hard or the egg will crush in your hand. (Yuck.) Hold the egg over the bowl, cracked side down, and with your thumbs pull the two sides of the shell apart and let the egg flow into the bowl underneath. Remove any bits of eggshell with the tip of a spoon or the corner of a slice of bread.

Separate the Egg Yolk and Egg White

To separate the white part from the yellow part of the egg, start with an egg right out of the refrigerator, so it's cold. Wash your hands, then crack the egg, following the directions above, into a bowl. Be gentle, though, so the yolk doesn't spread into the white. Cup one hand, with your fingers only slightly apart. Slip your cupped hand under the yolk and gently lift it out of the bowl, allowing the white to flow through your fingers. Discard the yolk or put it into a small bowl, cover with plastic wrap, and refrigerate. Or ask an adult to show you how to transfer the yolk back and forth from shell half to shell half to separate the white from the yellow; it is much easier to learn this technique by watching someone else than by reading directions.

Dice and Slice Foods

Dicing and slicing with a small knife is easier if the knife is sharp. But that means you must be very, very careful. Grip the handle with your writing hand. With your other hand, hold the food that you will be slicing (hold it steady, so the knife doesn't slip). Cut or slice the food by pressing down and pulling the knife toward you. Always use a cutting board when dicing and slicing.

Grate Foods

You will need a food grater for some of these recipes. You can use a four-sided grater with a handle or a one-sided grater. Use the large holes for vegetables and soft cheeses. Place a cutting board or some wax paper under the grater to catch the food when it falls. Hold the food in your writing hand and grasp the handle of the grater with the other hand. Move the food from top to bottom over the teeth of the grater and back up again in a continuous motion. Watch your fingertips and knuckles because the teeth of the grater are very sharp and can cause a nasty cut. Be careful!

Measure Dry Ingredients

Place dry ingredients, such as flour, granulated sugar, baking powder, baking soda, or cornmeal, in the correct measuring cup or spoon. Level the ingredients by placing the straight edge of a butter knife against the rim of the cup or spoon. Move the knife along the rim until all of the excess ingredient is removed.

Measure Liquid Ingredients

Pour liquids into a glass measuring cup and measure at eye level. When the amount is small, pour the ingredient into a measuring spoon until the spoon is full.

Core Apples

Wash the apple and place it on a cutting board. Using a small, sharp knife, slice the apple in half, cutting lengthwise through the stem. Place the two halves cut side down and slice each in half again. You'll now have four wedges. Remove the seeds and core with the knife.

BREAKFAST

Terrific Toast
Banana Split Cereal
Oaty-Meal
Blueberry Pancakes
Bananany Bread
Heart-Happy French Toast
English Muf-faces
Sizzling Grapefruit
Apple Wake-Me-Up
Blueberry Muffins
Pineapple Bran Muffins

TERRIFIC TOAST

When your breakfast has got to be quick, this recipe is the pick!

Serves 1   Rookie

TOOLS:

measuring spoon
measuring cup
butter knife
small, sharp knife
cutting board
spatula

INGREDIENTS:

¹/₄ washed apple (or a
    fresh peach or pear)
1 slice whole-wheat or
    other whole-grain
    bread
¹/₄ cup low-fat cottage
    cheese
1 tablespoon raisins
Cinnamon

Whole-wheat flour is rich in dietary fiber, vitamins, and minerals. When you buy wheat bread, check the ingredients and make sure "whole-wheat flour" is the *only* flour.

DIRECTIONS:

1. Cut away the stem and core from the apple. Slice it into very thin wedges.

2. Toast the bread lightly in a toaster or toaster oven.

3. Remove the bread. Place it on a flat pan that will fit in your toaster oven or under the broiler of a regular oven. Spread the cottage cheese on the toast with the butter knife.

4. Top the cheese with the raisins. Layer the apple slices over the raisins and cheese and sprinkle with cinnamon.

5. Return the bread to the toaster oven or place on the shelf of the oven closest to the broiler. Broil for about 4 or 5 minutes and remove carefully with a spatula.

Per serving: Calories: 159; Total Fat: 1.7 grams (.4 teaspoons); Saturated Fat: 0.8 grams; Sodium: 411 milligrams; Cholesterol: 3 milligrams.

BANANA SPLIT CEREAL

Who said banana splits were only for dessert? Yogurt, cereal, and fruit combine to make a powerhouse breakfast!

Serves 1   Rookie

TOOLS:

small, sharp knife
measuring cup
spoon
colander
cutting board

INGREDIENTS:

1 small, ripe banana
½ cup fresh blueberries or
    other fresh fruit
½ cup nonfat or low-fat
    vanilla yogurt
½ cup low-sugar cereal
    (such as Cheerios,
    Wheaties, Grape-
    Nuts, or Bran Flakes)

DIRECTIONS:

1. Peel the banana and slice it lengthwise (from tip to tip). Wash the blueberries by placing them in a colander and running water over them. (If you are using another fruit, wash it and cut it into small pieces.)

2. Spoon the yogurt in a mound in the center of a cereal bowl.

3. Sprinkle the cereal on top of the yogurt.

4. Arrange the banana halves on either side of the yogurt.

5. Sprinkle the top with the blueberries or other fruit.

Per serving: Calories: 279; Total Fat: 2.7 grams (.6 teaspoons); Saturated Fat: 0.5 grams; Sodium: 246 milligrams; Cholesterol: 2 milligrams.

OATY-MEAL

Put a little zip into your hot cereal. Try this recipe using apples, raisins, and cinnamon.

Makes about 1 cup   Intermediate

TOOLS:

measuring spoons
measuring cups
small, sharp knife
cutting board
small pan with lid (big
    enough to hold 2
    cups)
long-handled wooden
    spoon

INGREDIENTS:

$^3/_4$ cup water
$^1/_3$ cup old-fashioned oats
$^1/_2$ washed apple
$^1/_4$ cup skim milk
1 tablespoon raisins or
    chopped dates
$^1/_8$ teaspoon cinnamon

Make time for a good breakfast; it will keep your motor running until lunch! Oatmeal has dietary fiber, protein, and vitamins, but almost no fat or sugar.

DIRECTIONS:

1. Place the water in a small pan. Bring to a boil (bubbles). Add the oats and reduce the heat to low. Cook for 5 minutes, stirring occasionally. (Remember to hold the handle of the pan with oven mitts while stirring.)

2. Cover the pan and remove from the heat.

3. Cut away the stem and core from the apple. Cut the half into small chunks.

4. Add the milk, apple, raisins or dates, and cinnamon to the oatmeal. Stir to combine.

5. Dish up the oatmeal into a cereal bowl and enjoy!

Per 1-cup serving: Calories: 198; Total Fat: 1.8 grams (.4 teaspoons); Saturated Fat: 0.4 grams; Sodium: 34 milligrams; Cholesterol: 1 milligram.

BLUEBERRY PANCAKES

Try these berry-licious pancakes on weekend or holiday mornings when you have extra time for breakfast.

Makes 12 pancakes   Master

TOOLS:

large, nonstick frying pan
  or griddle
wire whisk
long-handled wooden
  spoon
large mixing bowl
spatula
measuring cups
measuring spoons
medium mixing bowl

INGREDIENTS:

$\frac{1}{2}$ cup all-purpose flour
$\frac{1}{2}$ cup whole-wheat flour
$1\frac{1}{2}$ teaspoons baking
  powder
$\frac{1}{2}$ teaspoon baking soda
1 cup buttermilk
1 egg
1 egg white
1 tablespoon vegetable oil
1 cup blueberries, fresh or
  frozen (if frozen,
  there is no need to
  thaw the berries
  completely before
  using them)
Vegetable oil spray
Fresh fruit, fruit spread, or
  light syrup

DIRECTIONS:

1. In a large bowl, mix the flours, baking powder, and baking soda with a wooden spoon (about 10 circles).

2. In a medium bowl, whip the buttermilk, egg, egg white, and oil with a wire whisk until it is fluffy and a light yellow (about 30 quick strokes).

3. Add the wet ingredients to the dry flour mixture. Whip with the wire whisk until it is combined but not smooth (about 20 brisk strokes)—it should be a little bit lumpy.

4. Add the blueberries and *gently* mix them into the batter using the wooden spoon.

5. Heat a large, nonstick frying pan or griddle to medium-hot (350 degrees). Spray with vegetable oil spray. Drop a tiny drop of the batter into the frying pan to test for the correct heat—when it sizzles it is ready. Pour ¼ cup of batter into the frying pan. When the pancake is all bubbly on top and the edges are starting to brown lightly, carefully flip the pancake using a spatula. Cook on this side for 1 or 2 minutes.

6. Serve the pancakes immediately, with your favorite fresh fruit, fruit spread, or light syrup.

Per pancake: Calories: 68; Total Fat: 2.1 grams (.5 teaspoons); Saturated Fat: 0.4 grams; Sodium: 103 milligrams; Cholesterol: 24 milligrams.

When you use syrup, dribble on just a small amount. You'll still enjoy the taste, but cut out some extra sugar! Syrup contains sugar and water, no vitamins or minerals.

BANANANY BREAD

Bake this bread after supper and eat it the next morning with a glass of skim milk and a piece of fruit for a quick and healthy breakfast.

Serves 8   Intermediate

TOOLS:

large mixing bowl
long-handled wooden
    spoon
measuring spoons
butter knife
8-inch round pan
wire rack
medium mixing bowl
small, sharp knife
measuring cups
cutting board
electric mixer or food
    processor
toothpick
timer

INGREDIENTS:

Vegetable oil spray
3 medium-size, brown-
    speckled bananas,
    each 6 inches long
2 egg whites
$^3/_4$ cup whole-wheat flour
$^3/_4$ cup all-purpose flour
2 teaspoons baking
    powder
$^1/_2$ teaspoon baking soda
$^1/_4$ teaspoon nutmeg
$^1/_2$ cup honey
$^1/_2$ cup skim milk
$1^1/_2$ teaspoons vanilla
    extract
2 tablespoons vegetable oil

"Bananas have a lot of the mineral potassium, which helps keep me in tip-top condition."

16

DIRECTIONS:

1. Preheat the oven to 400 degrees and lightly grease a round pan by spraying it with vegetable oil spray.

2. Peel the bananas and slice them into large chunks. Put the banana chunks into a large bowl. Add the egg whites. Using an electric mixer or food processor, beat the bananas and egg whites until the mixture is smooth and a light yellow (about 4 minutes).

3. In a medium bowl, combine the flours, baking powder, baking soda, and nutmeg. Stir with a wooden spoon to mix them.

4. Add the flour mixture, honey, milk, vanilla, and oil to the large bowl with the banana mixture. Beat with the electric mixer on medium speed or in the food processor until it is smooth.

5. Pour or scoop the batter into the prepared pan.

6. Put on your oven mitts and open the oven door. Place the pan in the middle of the center rack.

7. Set the timer and bake the bread for 40 minutes or until a wooden toothpick inserted into the center comes out clean.

8. When the bread is done, put your oven mitts back on and place the hot pan on a wire rack to cool for about 30 minutes. Remove the bread from the pan by sliding a butter knife around the edges of the bread between the bread and the pan. Then turn the pan upside down and the bread should fall out. If it doesn't fall out immediately, let the bread cool upside down.

Per serving: Calories: 228; Total Fat: 4.2 grams (1 teaspoon); Saturated Fat: 0.5 grams; Sodium: 147 milligrams; Cholesterol: 0 milligrams.

HEART-HAPPY
FRENCH TOAST

When you want to impress your family with a sample of your cooking skills, try this recipe for Sunday brunch.

Serves 4   Intermediate

TOOLS:

medium mixing bowl
egg beater or fork or wire
    whisk
spatula
measuring cup
measuring spoons
large, nonstick frying pan
    or griddle
dinner plate

INGREDIENTS:

3 egg whites
1 egg
½ cup skim milk
2 tablespoons orange
    juice
1 teaspoon brown sugar
¼ teaspoon vanilla extract
8 slices whole-wheat
    bread
Margarine
Fresh fruit, fruit spread, or
    light syrup
Cinnamon

DIRECTIONS:

1. In a medium bowl, whip the egg whites, egg, milk, and juice using an egg beater, a fork, or a wire whisk (about 20 strokes).

2. Add the sugar and vanilla and beat until slightly foamy (about 15 strokes).

3. Dip the bread, a slice at a time, into the egg mixture. Flip it to coat both sides, then place the bread on a dinner plate. Repeat this until all the bread is coated.

4. Over medium-high temperature (350 degrees), heat a small amount of margarine on a griddle or in a large frying pan. Spread the margarine around using the tip of a spatula. Cook the coated bread until the underside is golden brown, about 2 minutes (lift up the corner of the bread with the spatula to check). Flip the bread onto the other side and cook for another 2 minutes.

5. Serve the toast warm with your favorite fresh fruit, fruit spread, or light syrup, and a sprinkle of cinnamon.

Per 2-slice serving: Calories: 194; Total Fat: 3.6 grams (.8 teaspoons); Saturated Fat: 1.3 grams; Sodium: 431 milligrams; Cholesterol: 69 milligrams.

"My yolk is high in cholesterol. This recipe doesn't use a lot of egg yolks. It has only one-fourth of the cholesterol that most other French toast recipes have. This will keep your heart happy!"

ENGLISH MUF-FACES

Transform plain English muffins into a fun-filled breakfast.

Serves 1   Rookie

TOOLS:

butter knife
small, sharp knife
cutting board
measuring spoon

INGREDIENTS:

1 English muffin (whole-
    wheat, if possible)
1 tablespoon peanut
    butter
$\frac{1}{2}$ banana
4 raisins
2 small strawberries or
    grapes
2 orange sections

**"I taste just fine and that is true,
but I'm high in fat, so don't overdo!"**

DIRECTIONS:

1. Split the muffin in half and place the halves in a toaster or toaster oven. Toast until golden brown.

2. Put your oven mitts on to remove the toasted muffins. Spread half the peanut butter with a butter knife on each muffin half while it is still warm.

3. Cut the banana into disks. Set aside 4 and snack on the rest.

4. Make a face on each muffin by using 2 banana disks topped with 1 raisin each as the eyes, 1 strawberry or grape for a nose, and 1 orange section for a mouth.

Per serving: Calories: 336; Total Fat: 9.6 grams (2.2 teaspoons); Saturated Fat: 1.8 grams; Sodium: 277 milligrams; Cholesterol: 0 milligrams.

SIZZLING GRAPEFRUIT

Try this recipe before you eat your bowl of cereal in the morning.

Serves 2   Rookie

TOOLS:

small, sharp knife
grapefruit knife
cutting board
measuring spoon
timer

INGREDIENTS:

1 grapefruit
2 teaspoons apple juice
Cinnamon

Quiz time: What vitamin in grapefruit is needed by the body for healing wounds and growing strong bones, teeth, and muscles?

Answer: Vitamin C.

DIRECTIONS:

1. Position the grapefruit on the cutting board so the sides with the buttonlike marks face left and right. Grasp one of the sides of the grapefruit to hold it steady. Place the small, sharp knife directly in the middle of the grapefruit and slice down to the cutting board.

2. Use a grapefruit knife to cut around inside the skin of each half to loosen the juicy fruit. Make deep cuts between the grapefruit pieces close to the membranes dividing them.

3. Place the grapefruit halves, cut side up, on the broiler pan.

4. Sprinkle 1 teaspoon of apple juice on the top of each grapefruit half. Spread it with your finger to evenly cover the top of the fruit.

5. Sprinkle cinnamon on the top of each grapefruit half.

6. Turn the broiler on. Put your oven mitts on and very carefully place the broiler pan with the grapefruit halves on it about 4 inches from the heat. Set the timer and broil the grapefruit for 6 to 8 minutes.

7. Put your oven mitts back on to remove the broiler pan from the oven. Serve the grapefruit while it is still warm.

Per Serving: Calories: 42; Total Fat: 0 grams; Saturated Fat: 0 grams; Sodium: 1 milligram; Cholesterol: 0 milligrams.

APPLE WAKE-ME-UP

Have this apple dish with a glass of milk and whole-wheat toast, and you are ready to roll!

Serves 1 (or 2 smaller servings)   Intermediate

TOOLS:

measuring cups
small pan with lid (big
   enough to hold 2
   cups)
wire rack or hot pad
measuring spoons
small, sharp knife
cutting board

INGREDIENTS:

1 large apple, unpeeled
$1/3$ cup apple juice
1 tablespoon raisins
$1/4$ cup Grape-Nuts cereal
   (not the flakes)
$1^1/2$ teaspoons maple
   syrup
$1/2$ teaspoon cinnamon

Quiz time: You need vitamin C. Do cats and dogs?

Answer: No. Their bodies can make vitamin C. Only people, monkeys, guinea pigs, and a few other animals need vitamin C.

DIRECTIONS:

1. Wash the apple, cut it in half, and remove the stem and core. Cut the apple into small chunks and place them in a small pan.

2. Add the apple juice and raisins to the pan and cook on the stove over medium heat until it boils (bubbles). Cover the pan, turn down the heat a little, and let it boil slowly for 5 minutes.

3. Using a pot holder and both hands, remove the pan from the stove and place on a wire rack or hot pad. Stir in the cereal, syrup, and cinnamon and let the mixture stand for another 5 minutes to cool before you eat it.

Per serving: Calories: 277; Total Fat: less than 1 gram; Saturated Fat: 0.1 gram; Sodium: 206 milligrams; Cholesterol: 0 milligrams.

BLUEBERRY MUFFINS

These muffins will be gobbled up before you know it!

Makes 12 muffins   Intermediate

TOOLS:

12-cup muffin tin
measuring cups
wire rack
large mixing bowl
long-handled wooden
    spoon
toothpick
measuring spoons
timer
medium mixing bowl
electric mixer or egg
    beater
spoon

INGREDIENTS:

Vegetable oil spray
1 cup all-purpose flour
1 cup whole-wheat flour
1 teaspoon baking powder
$\frac{1}{2}$ teaspoon baking soda
$\frac{1}{4}$ teaspoon salt
2 tablespoons vegetable oil
1 cup low-fat buttermilk
2 egg whites
$\frac{1}{3}$ cup honey
1 teaspoon vanilla extract
1 cup blueberries, fresh or
    frozen

DIRECTIONS:

1. Preheat the oven to 350 degrees. Lightly grease the muffin cups by spraying them with vegetable oil spray.

2. In a large bowl, combine the flours, baking powder, baking soda, and salt. Mix with a wooden spoon.

3. In a medium bowl, combine the oil, buttermilk, egg whites, honey, and vanilla. Mix with an electric mixer on low speed or with an egg beater until the ingredients are completely combined and the mixture is smooth (about 2 minutes).

4. Add the wet ingredients in the medium bowl to the large bowl with the flour mixture. Mix with the electric mixer on

medium speed or by hand with the wooden spoon until it is a smooth batter, about 3 or 4 minutes.

5. Add the blueberries to the batter and gently mix with the wooden spoon until the fruit is evenly combined.

6. Spoon the batter into the greased muffin tin, filling each cup almost to the top.

7. Put on your oven mitts and open the oven door. Place the muffin tin in the middle of the center rack. Set the timer and bake the muffins for about 25 minutes or until a toothpick inserted into the center of one of the muffins in the middle of the pan comes out clean.

8. When the muffins are done, put your oven mitts back on and place the muffin tin on a wire rack to cool for 15 minutes. Remove the muffins from the tin.

Per muffin: Calories: 136; Total Fat: 2.9 grams (.7 teaspoons); Saturated Fat: 0.4 grams; Sodium: 135 milligrams; Cholesterol: 1 milligram.

Did the name "buttermilk" fool you into thinking that buttermilk is made from high-fat butter? Truth is, it is made from low-fat milk, making it a good-for-you food.

PINEAPPLE BRAN
MUFFINS

These muffins don't have to be limited to breakfast time—
they are excellent for snack time, too.

Makes 12 muffins   Intermediate

TOOLS:

12-cup muffin tin
measuring cups
wire rack
small mixing bowl
medium mixing bowl
large mixing bowl
long-handled wooden
      spoon
measuring spoons
timer
egg beater
paper towels
spoon

INGREDIENTS:

Vegetable oil spray
½ cup all-purpose flour
½ cup whole-wheat flour
2 teaspoons baking
      powder
½ teaspoon baking soda
1 teaspoon cinnamon
1½ cups bran cereal
      (such as All Bran or
      100% Bran)
½ cup skim milk
½ cup plain low-fat yogurt
1 egg
1 tablespoon vegetable oil
¼ cup honey
¾ cup juice-packed
      crushed pineapple,
      drained and liquid
      discarded

Ever wonder why store-bought muffins are moist? The answer
is fat (about 1 or 2 teaspoons for each muffin). These homemade muffins have only ½ teaspoon of fat each but are moist
because of the pineapple.

DIRECTIONS:

1. Preheat the oven to 400 degrees. Lightly grease the muffin cups by spraying them with vegetable oil spray.

2. With a wooden spoon, stir together the flours, baking powder, baking soda, and cinnamon in a medium bowl. Set the mixture aside.

3. Put the bran cereal in a large bowl and add the milk and yogurt. Stir with the wooden spoon until well mixed (about 20 circles), then let the mixture stand until the bran softens and looks mushy, about 1 or 2 minutes.

4. In a small bowl, whip the egg, oil, and honey with an egg beater. Add this whipped mixture to the bran. Stir well with the wooden spoon until it is thoroughly combined (about 25 circles).

5. Pour the flour mixture into the bran-egg mixture. Stir until the dry ingredients are completely wet (about 20 circles, making sure to scrape the sides of the bowl). Add the pineapple to the bran mixture and stir again until the pineapple is mixed in evenly.

6. Spoon the batter into the cups, almost to the top.

7. Put your oven mitts on and open the oven door. Place the muffin tin in the middle of the center rack. Set the oven timer for 20 minutes.

8. Set up your cooling area by placing a wire rack on the counter. Put some paper towels under the rack to catch the crumbs.

9. When the timer goes off, use your mitts to place the muffin tin on the wire rack to cool for 15 minutes.

10. Remove the muffins from the tin and place them on the wire rack to continue cooling.

Per muffin: Calories: 112; Total Fat: 2.2 grams (.5 teaspoons); Saturated Fat: 0.4 grams; Sodium: 182 milligrams; Cholesterol: 24 milligrams.

LUNCH

Soups

Pancho's Gazpacho
Super Veggie Soup

Sandwiches/Entrées

Muffin Pizzas
Tempting Tuna
Fruit-n-Nut Sandwich Filling
Soft Bean-and-Cheese Tacos
Oodles of Sandwiches

Salads

Cucumber Boats
Chicken Fruit Salad
Fruity Carrot Slaw
Mouse-in-the-House Salad
Granny Smith Salad

Side Dishes

Corn Cakes
Spuds

PANCHO'S GAZPACHO

This cold tomato soup from Spain is great on a hot afternoon.

Serves 4   Intermediate

TOOLS:

large serving bowl
cutting board
measuring cup
blender or food processor
small, sharp knife
measuring spoons
can opener

"I'm a zippy soup rich in vitamins A and C and fat-free!"

INGREDIENTS:

3 tomatoes
1 medium-size green
    pepper
1 celery stalk, about 5 to 6
    inches long
2 scallions (green onions)
2 garlic cloves
1 16-ounce can whole
    tomatoes, no salt
    added
1 cup chilled tomato juice
2 tablespoons wine vinegar
1 tablespoon chopped
    fresh parsley *or* 1
    teaspoon dried
    parsley
1/8 teaspoon hot pepper
    sauce, such as
    Tabasco
1/8 teaspoon black pepper

DIRECTIONS:

1. Wash the tomatoes, green pepper, celery, and scallions.

2. Slice the tomatoes in half and remove the core. Cut the tomatoes into small chunks and place in a large serving bowl.

3. Cut the green pepper in half lengthwise and remove the stem and seeds. Wash the halves and cut them into small chunks. Add the chunks to the serving bowl.

4. Chop the celery into very small pieces and place in the serving bowl.

5. Slice off the very bottoms of the scallions and remove any of the green leaves that look brown or yellow. Slice the scallions into thin slices (about 1/4 inch) and place in the serving bowl with the rest of the vegetables.

6. Peel the garlic and chop it up as fine as you can, then place in the serving bowl.

7. Open the can of tomatoes and pour the tomatoes with their liquid and the chilled tomato juice into a blender or food processor. Puree until well blended, about 3 minutes.

8. Add the pureed tomatoes, vinegar, parsley, pepper sauce, and black pepper to the serving bowl and stir until everything is mixed together.

9. Serve the soup chilled (the bowl should feel slightly cold when you put your hands on the bottom). If necessary, set the bowl in the refrigerator to chill for 15 to 20 minutes before eating.

Per serving: Calories: 61; Total Fat: less than 1 gram; Saturated Fat: 0.1 gram; Sodium: 253 milligrams; Cholesterol: 0 milligrams.

SUPER VEGGIE SOUP

Once you taste homemade soup, you won't go back to canned.

Serves 6   Master

TOOLS:

cutting board
measuring cups
vegetable peeler
large soup pot with lid
small, sharp knife
can opener
long-handled wooden
    spoon
2-quart pan with lid
hot pad
measuring spoons
timer

The big difference between this soup and canned is S-A-L-T. This soup has far less salt than canned or instant. Check ingredient lists for salt (sodium chloride) and other sodium-containing ingredients.

INGREDIENTS:

1³/₄ cups plus 2
    tablespoons water
¹/₂ cup brown rice
    (uncooked)
1 medium-size green
    pepper
1 small onion
1 celery stalk, about 5 to 6
    inches long
1 yellow squash, about 5
    to 6 inches long
2 medium-size carrots,
    about 5 to 6 inches
    long
1 tablespoon olive oil or
    vegetable oil
2¹/₂ cups chicken broth,
    homemade or low-
    sodium canned
1 tablespoon chopped
    fresh basil *or* 1
    teaspoon dried basil
1 tablespoon chopped
    fresh parsley *or* 1
    teaspoon dried
    parsley
¹/₂ teaspoon black pepper

34

DIRECTIONS:

1. Place 1³/₄ cups water in a 2-quart pan and bring the water to a boil. Add the brown rice. Cover the pan tightly and cook over low heat. Set the timer for 50 minutes.

2. Cut the pepper in half lengthwise and remove the stem and seeds. Wash the pepper and chop it into small pieces.

3. Cut the ends off of the onion, peel away the outer skin, and chop the onion into small pieces.

4. Wash the celery and squash, cut off the very tops and bottoms, and chop the celery and squash into bite-size pieces.

5. Cut off the tops of the carrots, peel them, and slice them into coin-size pieces.

6. Place the oil in a large pot and turn the heat to medium. Add the chopped vegetables and the remaining 2 table-spoons of water. Cook the vegetables, stirring occasionally with a wooden spoon, until they are soft.

7. Add the chicken broth, basil, parsley, and black pepper. Stir to mix everything together. Place the pot on the stove over medium-high heat and bring the mixture to a boil.

8. Reduce the heat to low, cover the pot, and cook for 30 minutes.

9. Add the cooked brown rice. Stir with the wooden spoon to combine the ingredients and cook on low heat for another 5 minutes. Using pot holders and both hands, remove the pot from the stove and place on a hot pad. Serve immediately.

Per serving: Calories: 117; Total Fat: 3.8 grams (.9 teaspoons); Saturated Fat: 0.6 grams; Sodium: 46 milligrams; Cholesterol: 0 milligrams.

MUFFIN PIZZAS

Be a pizza whiz by preparing these miniature pizzas in minutes.

Serves 2   Intermediate

TOOLS:

cutting board
small, sharp knife
measuring spoons
small bowl
paper towels
can opener

"Pssst, want my secret for delicious pizza that's good for you? Use low-fat toppings like vegetables, and go easy on the cheese, which is usually high in fat."

INGREDIENTS:

2 English muffins (whole-
    wheat, if possible)
1 small onion
4 fresh mushrooms
2 tablespoons canned
    tomato paste, no salt
    added
2 tablespoons water
1/2 teaspoon dried oregano
Black pepper (optional)
4 thin slices part-skim
    mozzarella cheese

DIRECTIONS:

1. Slice or separate the muffins into halves and place them in a toaster or toaster oven. Toast until the muffins are golden brown.

2. While the muffins are toasting, cut the ends off of the onion and peel away the outer skin. Chop the onion into little pieces (smaller than a raisin).

3. Wipe the mushrooms with a damp paper towel and slice off the very end part of each stem. Slice the mushrooms as thin as you can.

4. Make a tomato sauce by mixing the tomato paste, water, and oregano in a small bowl. Add a dash of black pepper for a spicier pizza.

5. Put your oven mitts on and place the toasted muffins on the broiler pan.

6. Top each with 1 tablespoon of the tomato sauce. Sprinkle with the onions and mushrooms and place a slice of cheese on top.

7. Put your oven mitts back on and place the pizzas under the broiler (of a stove or toaster oven), about 4 inches away from the heat. Broil until the cheese melts, about 4 or 5 minutes.

Per pizza: Calories: 279; Total Fat: 8.7 grams (2 teaspoons); Saturated Fat: 4.9 grams; Sodium: 447 milligrams; Cholesterol: 23 milligrams.

TEMPTING TUNA

Having tuna for lunch is fast, nutritious, and delicious.

Serves 4   Intermediate

TOOLS:

can opener
small, sharp knife
cutting board
vegetable peeler
spoon
medium mixing bowl
colander
measuring spoon

INGREDIENTS:

1 6½-ounce can tuna,
    packed in water
1 small carrot, about 5
    inches long
1 small celery stalk, about
    5 to 7 inches long
3 tablespoons plain nonfat
    or low-fat yogurt
1 tablespoon lemon juice
4 whole-grain rolls

Fat-Saver Tip: Tuna packed
in water has about one-
seventh as much fat as tuna
packed in oil.

DIRECTIONS:

1. Open the can of tuna. Be careful with the lid! Place the tuna in a colander. Wash the tuna with water (no soap, please!) for 1 minute to remove most of the salt.
2. Put the drained tuna in a medium bowl.
3. Peel the carrot and wash the celery and cut off the tops and bottoms of both. Cut the carrot and celery into small pieces (about the size of a pencil eraser). Add the carrots and celery to the tuna.
4. Add the yogurt and lemon juice to the tuna. Mix well with a spoon until the ingredients are evenly coated with the yogurt and there are no big "clumps" of tuna.
5. Spread on whole-grain rolls and serve.

Per serving: Calories: 188; Total Fat: 2 grams (.5 teaspoons); Saturated Fat: 0.8 grams; Sodium: 352 milligrams; Cholesterol: 24 milligrams. (Note: Nutritional analysis based on rinsed tuna.)

FRUIT-N-NUT
SANDWICH FILLING

A yummy lunch-box feast!

Serves 4   Rookie

TOOLS:

medium mixing bowl
cutting board
spoon
measuring cup
long-handled wooden
    spoon
small, sharp knife

INGREDIENTS:

1 orange
1 medium-size banana
$^1/_3$ cup raisins
$^1/_3$ cup crunchy peanut
    butter
8 slices whole-grain bread

High blood pressure is when the blood presses too hard against
a person's arteries—and it can injure him or her. If you exercise,
stay slim, and eat less salt, you can help protect your body from
this "pressure."

DIRECTIONS:

1. Peel the orange and separate the sections. Remove as much of the white lining (the pith) as you can. Cut each section into 3 or 4 pieces to fill ½ cup. Save any leftover orange for a snack.

2. Peel the banana and cut it in half crosswise. Cut half into small cubes and save the other half for a snack.

3. Place the orange, banana, raisins, and peanut butter in a medium bowl and mix thoroughly with a wooden spoon.

4. Spoon the filling evenly among 4 slices of bread and top with the other 4 slices to make sandwiches, or store whatever you don't use in the refrigerator in a tightly covered jar or container.

Per serving: Calories: 327; Total Fat: 12.8 grams (2.9 teaspoons); Saturated Fat: 2.7 grams; Sodium: 461 milligrams; Cholesterol: 0 milligrams.

SOFT BEAN-
AND-CHEESE TACOS

This recipe uses corn tortillas, but you can substitute flour tortillas if they are your favorite.

Serves 3   Intermediate

TOOLS:

aluminum foil
cutting board
can opener
measuring cups
medium mixing bowl
food grater
small, sharp knife
potato masher or fork
4 small bowls

INGREDIENTS:

6 soft corn tortillas
A chunk of Monterey Jack
  cheese
1 cup home-cooked or
  canned pinto or
  kidney beans
3 medium-size tomatoes
  (about 1 pound)
1 medium-size onion
1 cup chopped lettuce
$\frac{1}{2}$ cup bottled salsa

DIRECTIONS:

1. Wrap the tortillas in aluminum foil and place them in the middle of the center rack. Set the oven to 275 degrees. This will make the tortillas soft and warm.

2. Grate the cheese, to fill $\frac{1}{3}$ cup, onto a cutting board. Use the side of the grater that has the large holes. Scrape the grated cheese into a small bowl.

3. Drain and wash the beans. Place them in a medium bowl. Mash the beans with a potato masher or fork until they look slightly lumpy.

4. Wash the tomatoes and remove the stems. Cut the tomatoes into bite-size pieces and place in a small bowl.

5. Cut the ends off of the onion and peel away the outer skin. Chop the onion into very small pieces and place in the bowl with the tomato. Toss with your fingers to mix them.

6. Place the chopped lettuce and the salsa in separate small bowls.

7. Put on your oven mitts and remove the warmed tortillas from the oven. Place the tortillas on dinner plates (2 for each plate). Spread 2 heaping tablespoons of beans on each tortilla, then top with the cheese, tomato and onion mixture, lettuce, and salsa. Fold the tortilla so that it fits easily in your hand.

Per 2-taco serving: Calories: 313; Total Fat: 7.2 grams (1.6 teaspoons); Saturated Fat: 3.0 grams; Sodium: 168 milligrams; Cholesterol: 14 milligrams.

Calories 228
Fat 2½ tsps.
Cholesterol 32 mgs.
Sodium 516 mgs.

FAST FOOD

Calories 156
Fat ⅘ tsps.
Cholesterol 7 mgs.
Sodium 84 mgs.

HOME MADE

Compare a fast-food taco with a soft taco made with this recipe.

OODLES OF SANDWICHES

A sandwich idea for every mood! Start your creation with two slices of whole-grain bread (oatmeal, whole-wheat, or multi-grain) or one whole-wheat pita bread and add one of the following fillings. Voilà! You are now a master of the fine art of healthy sandwich making. Now, on to the even more pleasing art of sandwich eating. . . .

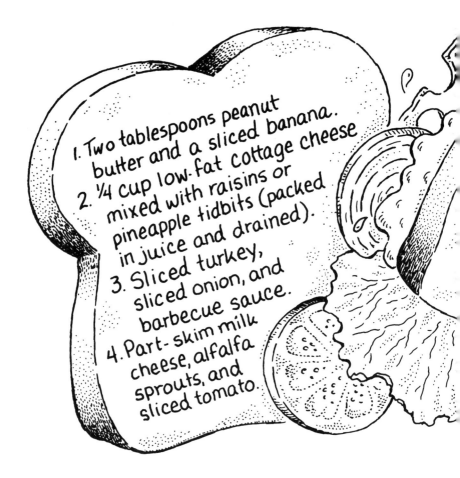

1. Two tablespoons peanut butter and a sliced banana.

2. ¼ cup low-fat cottage cheese mixed with raisins or pineapple tidbits (packed in juice and drained).

3. Sliced turkey, sliced onion, and barbecue sauce.

4. Part-skim milk cheese, alfalfa sprouts, and sliced tomato.

5. Hummus (see recipe in snack section of this book) and lettuce.
6. Sliced cucumbers, tomato, and onion with a thin spread of light mayonnaise.
7. Chopped, cooked chicken meat, mixed with chopped celery, low-fat yogurt, and a dash of black pepper.
8. Sliced turkey and cranberry sauce.
9. Smoked salmon, sliced onion, and a thin coating of light cream cheese.
10. Tuna (packed in water and drained) mixed with plain/nonfat or/low-fat yogurt and a dash of dijon mustard.

CUCUMBER BOATS

These boats may not float, but they sure taste great!

Serves 4   Intermediate

TOOLS:

can opener
measuring spoons
small mixing bowl
colander
small, sharp knife
vegetable peeler
cutting board
spoon

INGREDIENTS:

1 6½-ounce can tuna,
    packed in water
1 onion slice, about ¼
    inch thick
3 tablespoons plain nonfat
    or low-fat yogurt
1 teaspoon Dijon-style
    mustard (or any spicy
    mustard)
4 small cucumbers, about
    6 inches long
16 whole cloves

**"I'm low in calories, crispy,
cool, and juicy—just right
for a between-meal snack!"**

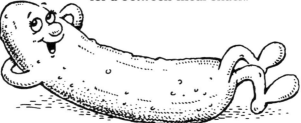

DIRECTIONS:

1. Open the can of tuna. Place the tuna in a colander and wash it with water to remove most of the salt. Drain the tuna well.

2. Cut the onion slice into very small pieces and measure 1 tablespoon of the chopped onion.

3. In a small bowl, combine the tuna, onion, yogurt, and mustard. Mix well until everything is combined.

4. Peel the cucumbers with a vegetable peeler.

5. Lay the cucumbers on a cutting board and make a lengthwise cut of $1/4$ inch off of one side of each. The cut should be deep enough to see the seeds. Scoop out the seeds of each cucumber with a spoon. Throw the seeds away.

6. Place the cucumbers cut side down and poke 4 cloves in the other side of each cucumber to act as feet so that the cucumbers will sit without rolling. You may have to experiment with this step since every cucumber has a slightly different shape. (Don't eat the cloves!)

7. Spoon the tuna into the well that you have created in the cucumber. Place the boat on a dish and serve.

Per serving: Calories: 94; Total Fat: less than 1 gram; Saturated Fat: 0.2 grams; Sodium: 94 milligrams; Cholesterol: 28 milligrams. (Note: Nutritional analysis based on rinsed tuna.)

CHICKEN FRUIT SALAD

A great way to use leftover chicken.

Serves 6   Intermediate

TOOLS:

large mixing bowl
cutting board
measuring cups
can opener
small mixing bowl
small, sharp knife
fork
measuring spoon
long-handled wooden
    spoon
plastic wrap

INGREDIENTS:

1 pound (or 4 breast
    halves) skinless,
    cooked chicken
1 celery stalk, about 5
    inches long
1 20-ounce can pineapple
    chunks, packed in
    juice
1 11-ounce can mandarin
    oranges, packed in
    light syrup
$3/4$ cup red or green
    seedless grapes
$1/4$ cup chopped walnuts
    or pecans
$1/4$ cup plain nonfat or
    low-fat yogurt
1 tablespoon mayonnaise
1 tablespoon lemon juice

Proteins are your body's building blocks. Nearly everything in your body contains protein—skin, muscles, hair, bones, teeth, and even your brain!

DIRECTIONS:

1. Cut the cooked chicken into bite-size cubes to fill 3 cups. Place the cubes in a large bowl.

2. Wash the celery and cut off the leaves on top. Chop the celery into small pieces (a little smaller than a raisin) and add it to the chicken.

3. Open the cans of pineapple and mandarin oranges and drain off the liquid. Place the fruit in the large bowl.

4. Wash the grapes and chop the nuts and place them in the large bowl.

5. Toss together the chicken, celery, pineapple, oranges, grapes, and nuts with a wooden spoon (or use your hands if they are clean!).

6. In a small bowl, mix the yogurt, mayonnaise, and lemon juice with a fork. Mix for 20 quick strokes.

7. Add the dressing to the chicken mixture and gently toss with the wooden spoon to coat the ingredients.

8. Cover the salad with plastic wrap or a tight-fitting lid and chill in the refrigerator for at least 1 hour. Serve with pita bread or whole-grain rolls for sandwiches, or by itself on a bed of lettuce.

Per serving: Calories: 251; Total Fat: 8.2 grams (1.9 teaspoons); Saturated Fat: 1.5 grams; Sodium: 83 milligrams; Cholesterol: 61 milligrams.

FRUITY CARROT SLAW

This salad adds a burst of color to a sandwich lunch.

Serves 6   Intermediate

TOOLS:

cutting board
measuring cups
small, sharp knife
medium mixing bowl
food grater
vegetable peeler
can opener
long-handled wooden
　　spoon

INGREDIENTS:

1 pound carrots (about 6
　　or 7 medium-size
　　carrots)
$1/2$ cup pineapple chunks,
　　packed in juice
$1/2$ cup raisins
$1/2$ cup orange juice
$1/4$ cup plain nonfat or
　　low-fat yogurt

"Hey, kids, crunch on a
carrot. They taste great and
are loaded with vitamin A,
which you need for good
vision. One carrot has more
than a day's worth of
vitamin A."

DIRECTIONS:

1. Peel the carrots and slice off the tops.

2. Grate the carrots onto the cutting board. Use the side of the grater that has the large holes.

3. Open the can of pineapple and drain off the liquid by pressing the lid against the pineapple and turning the can upside down over the sink.

4. Combine the grated carrots, pineapple, raisins, orange juice, and yogurt in a medium bowl. Mix with a wooden spoon until everything is coated with the yogurt.

5. Serve with your favorite soup or sandwich.

Per serving: Calories: 115; Total Fat: less than 1 gram; Saturated Fat: 0 grams; Sodium: 43 milligrams; Cholesterol: 0 milligrams.

MOUSE-IN-THE-HOUSE SALAD

A fun salad to make when you have friends over for lunch.

Serves 6   Rookie

TOOLS:

cutting board
vegetable peeler
paper towel
small, sharp knife
measuring cup
can opener

INGREDIENTS:

1 small carrot
1 large tomato
$\frac{1}{3}$ cup mung bean sprouts
    (about 30 sprouts)
6 lettuce leaves
6 thin slices part-skim
    mozzarella cheese
    (each about a 3-inch
    square)
6 canned pear halves in
    juice or light syrup,
    drained and liquid
    discarded
12 raisins

Swiss, American, and other hard cheeses are high in fat because they are made from whole milk. Choose "low-fat" or "reduced-fat" cheeses made from part-skim milk.

DIRECTIONS:

1. Peel the carrot and cut off the top and bottom. Slice 6 thin coins off the carrot. Cut the carrot coins in half and set them aside to be used later. Munch on the remaining carrot while you continue.

2. Wash the tomato and cut out the stem end. Cut the tomato into 6 round slices.

3. Wash the bean sprouts. Select 6 of the thickest and longest sprouts and set them aside to be used for the tails. Cut the root ends and the flower ends off of the remaining sprouts and trim them so they are even in length. These sprouts will be used for the whiskers.

4. Wash the lettuce leaves with cold water and pat them dry with a paper towel. Place 1 lettuce leaf each on salad plates.

5. Arrange a cheese slice on top of the lettuce. Place a tomato slice on top of the cheese and then a pear half on top of the tomato.

6. You are now ready to create the mice. Stick 1 sprout selected for the tails into the wider half of each pear. Stick 4 of the smaller sprouts at the thinner half of each pear for the whiskers. Push 2 raisins into each pear above the whiskers for the eyes. Push 2 of the halved carrot coins above the raisins for the ears.

Per serving: Calories: 121; Total Fat: 3.8 grams (.9 teaspoons); Saturated Fat: 2.4 grams; Sodium: 121 milligrams; Cholesterol: 13 milligrams.

GRANNY SMITH SALAD

A crisp salad to cool off a hot appetite. Eat it with a sandwich for a light lunch or serve it with your favorite soup.

Serves 4   Intermediate

TOOLS:

cutting board
measuring cup
vegetable peeler
small, sharp knife
food grater
medium mixing bowl
measuring spoons

INGREDIENTS:

1 large Granny Smith
    apple (tart green
    apple) *or* 2 small
    apples
1 teaspoon orange juice
1 carrot, about 5 inches
    long
2 tablespoons chopped
    walnuts
¼ cup plain nonfat or
    low-fat yogurt
¼ teaspoon cinnamon

Apples, carrots, and most other fruits and vegetables contain almost no fat. But walnuts and other nuts are high in fat and calories.

DIRECTIONS:

1. Wash the apple and cut it into 4 wedges. Carefully cut out the core and seeds. Cut the wedges into small cubes with the sharp knife and place them in a medium bowl.

2. Dribble the orange juice over the cut apples and toss to coat evenly with the juice. This prevents the apples from turning brown, and also adds a nice flavor.

3. Cut the top off the carrot, peel it, and grate it onto the cutting board. Use the side of the grater that has the large holes. Place the grated carrot in the bowl with the apple cubes.

4. Add the walnuts to the bowl.

5. Add the yogurt and cinnamon and toss until it is thoroughly mixed. Serve in small bowls.

Per serving: Calories: 80; Total Fat: 2.5 grams (.6 teaspoons); Saturated Fat: 0.3 grams; Sodium: 18 milligrams; Cholesterol: 0 milligrams.

CORN CAKES

These pancakes, made with a corn batter, taste great for a Saturday breakfast or lunch.

Makes 12 pancakes   Master

TOOLS:

large mixing bowl
small mixing bowl
measuring spoons
long-handled wooden
    spoon
measuring cups
egg beater
spatula
large nonstick frying pan
spoon

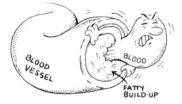

INGREDIENTS:

2 egg whites
1 egg
¼ cup skim milk
½ cup all-purpose flour
1 teaspoon baking powder
½ teaspoon sugar
2 cups cooked corn (cut
    from the cob, thawed
    frozen, or canned
    with the liquid
    drained)
¼ cup plain nonfat or
    low-fat yogurt
⅛ teaspoon nutmeg
2 tablespoons maple or
    maple-flavored syrup

Too much fat in your diet can make it a "tight squeeze" for your blood. These corn cakes are almost fat-free.

DIRECTIONS:

1. In a large mixing bowl, beat the egg whites with an egg beater until they are foamy.

2. Add to the same mixing bowl the egg, milk, flour, baking powder, and sugar. Stir together with a wooden spoon until the dry ingredients are mixed evenly into the wet ingredients.

3. Add the corn and stir until it is evenly combined with the batter.

4. Place the bowl in the refrigerator for about 30 minutes. During this time you can set the table, clean up your mess, and prepare the topping by mixing together the yogurt, nutmeg, and syrup in a small mixing bowl.

5. When 30 minutes is up, heat a frying pan to medium-high.

6. Drop the batter into the frying pan by large spoonfuls, to form 2-inch to 3-inch circles. Cook until the tops are full of holes and the edges begin to turn golden brown. Flip with the spatula and cook on the other side for about 1 minute. You can keep the pancakes warm in an oven set to 250 degrees while you are cooking the rest.

7. Serve with the yogurt topping.

Per corn cake: Calories: 65; Total Fat: less than 1 gram; Saturated Fat: 0.2 grams; Sodium: 47 milligrams; Cholesterol: 23 milligrams.

SPUDS

You can take your pick of toppings with this recipe!

Serves 4   Intermediate

TOOLS:

cutting board
cookie sheet
fork
small, sharp knife

INGREDIENTS:

4 Russet or Idaho
    potatoes, about 6
    ounces each

"Potatoes are packed with starch, which provides your body with fat-free energy!"

DIRECTIONS:

1. Preheat the oven to 375 degrees.

2. Wash the potatoes with warm water and scrub them to remove dirt from the skins. Poke holes in the potatoes with a fork.

3. Bake the potatoes for about 1 hour.

4. When they are cooked, carefully remove them from the oven with oven mitts. Place the potatoes on a cutting board and let them sit until they have cooled enough to handle—at least 10 minutes.

5. When cooled, cut the potatoes in half lengthwise. Squeeze the potatoes by placing your fingers on either side and pushing in. This should loosen up the insides of the potatoes. Using the fork, lightly mash up the insides and make a well in the center of each potato half. Fill each well with ¼ cup of any of the following toppings:

Ricotta Cheese and Spices Topping
Mix 2 cups part-skim ricotta cheese with ¼ teaspoon black pepper and ½ teaspoon dried parsley.

Per serving: Calories: 390; Total Fat: 9.7 grams (2.2 teaspoons); Saturated Fat: 6.2 grams; Sodium: 170 milligrams; Cholesterol: 38 milligrams.

Chili and Cheese Topping
Mix 1½ cups vegetarian baked beans with ¼ cup shredded part-skim mozzarella cheese.

Per serving: Calories: 326; Total Fat: 1.7 grams (.4 teaspoons); Saturated Fat: 0.9 grams; Sodium: 424 milligrams; Cholesterol: 4 milligrams. (Note: You can cut the sodium in this recipe by using plain canned beans that have been washed with water to remove the salt.)

Yogurt and Broccoli Topping
Mix 1 cup nonfat or low-fat plain yogurt with 1 cup cooked, chopped broccoli and ¼ teaspoon black pepper.

Per serving: Calories: 263; Total Fat: less than 1 gram; Saturated Fat: 0.2 grams; Sodium: 64 milligrams; Cholesterol: 1 milligram.

Cheese and Onion Topping

Mix 2 cups low-fat cottage cheese with one very finely chopped green onion.

Per serving: Calories: 302; Total Fat: 1.4 grams (.3 teaspoons); Saturated Fat: 0.9 grams; Sodium: 475 milligrams; Cholesterol: 5 milligrams. (Note: You can cut the sodium in this recipe in half by using 1 cup of dry-curd cottage cheese mixed with 1 cup of 1 percent cottage cheese.)

6. Place on the cookie sheet and return to the oven to warm for about 7 minutes.

SUPPER

Side Dishes

Sweet Potato Surprise
Dressed-Up Corn
Cucumber-Pepper Salad
Peppato Salad
Corny Bread

Main Dishes

Turkey Bar-B-Q
Lemon Chicken
Super Stir-fry
Fabulous Fish Sticks
Saucy Spaghetti
South-of-the-Border Casserole
Open Sesame Chicken
Beans-and-Veggies Chili
Deep-Sea Casserole

SWEET POTATO SURPRISE

This casserole is too delicious to limit to Thanksgiving Day.

Serves 6   Intermediate

TOOLS:

6- or 8-quart pot
fork
electric mixer
small, sharp knife
medium mixing bowl
hot pad or wire rack
colander
can opener
measuring cups
spatula
cutting board
2-quart baking dish
timer

INGREDIENTS:

1½ pounds fresh sweet
    potatoes (or canned
    sweet potatoes
    packed in water)
1 egg white
1 cup juice-packed
    crushed pineapple,
    drained and liquid
    discarded
⅓ cup pecans

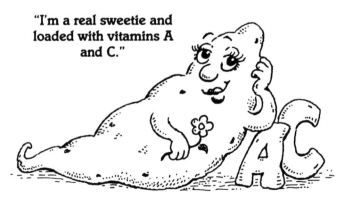

"I'm a real sweetie and
loaded with vitamins A
and C."

DIRECTIONS:

1. Preheat the oven to 350 degrees.

2. If using fresh potatoes, put them in a large pot, cover with water, and cook over medium-high heat. Boil the potatoes until you can easily pierce them with a fork, about 35 minutes. Dump them into a colander that has been placed in the sink, then cool them with cold running water. When the potatoes are cool enough to handle, slip the skins off with your fingers.

3. If using canned potatoes, open the can and drain off the water by holding the lid tightly against the potatoes and turning the can upside down over the sink.

4. Place the potatoes, egg white, and crushed pineapple in a medium bowl. Beat the ingredients with an electric mixer on medium speed until everything is well mixed, about 5 or 6 minutes.

5. Place the potato mixture in a baking dish. Smooth the top with a spatula.

6. Roughly chop the pecans on the cutting board, then sprinkle them over the top of the sweet potatoes.

7. Put your oven mitts on, open the oven door, and place the dish in the middle of the center rack. Set the timer and bake the sweet potato mixture for 30 minutes. When done, place the dish on a hot pad or wire rack to cool.

Per serving: Calories: 180; Total Fat: 4.5 grams (1 teaspoon); Saturated Fat: 0.4 grams; Sodium: 92 milligrams; Cholesterol: 0 milligrams. (Note: Nutritional analysis based on canned sweet potatoes.)

DRESSED-UP CORN

Golden yellow corn mixed with green peppers and orange carrots creates a bright vegetable side dish.

Serves 4   Intermediate

TOOLS:

cutting board
measuring spoons
long-handled wooden
    spoon
vegetable peeler
small, sharp knife
large frying pan with lid
food grater
wax paper

INGREDIENTS:

1 medium-size green
    pepper
1 tomato
1 carrot
1 teaspoon olive or
    safflower oil
1 10-ounce bag frozen
    corn
1 tablespoon water
Black pepper

DIRECTIONS:

1. Cut the pepper in half lengthwise and remove the stem and seeds. Wash the halves and chop them into small pieces (a tiny bit larger than a kernel of corn).

2. Wash the tomato and remove the stem end. Cut the tomato into small cubes.

3. Peel the carrot, cut off the top and bottom, and grate it over wax paper using the large holes of a grater.

4. Place the oil in a frying pan and turn the heat to medium. Immediately put the green pepper in the pan and cook for 5 minutes.

5. Add the tomato, carrots, frozen corn, and water and stir with a wooden spoon. Cover the pan and cook for 15 minutes. Add a dash of pepper before serving.

Per serving: Calories: 86; Total Fat: 1.3 grams (.3 teaspoons); Saturated Fat: 0.2 grams; Sodium: 13 milligrams; Cholesterol: 0 milligrams.

Quiz time: What sweet-tasting, fiber-rich vegetable did the native American Indians teach us how to grow, and is now the most widely grown American crop?

Answer: Corn.

CUCUMBER-PEPPER
SALAD

This salad is as "cool as a cucumber"!

Serves 4   Intermediate

TOOLS:

cutting board
measuring spoons
medium mixing bowl
small, sharp knife
vegetable peeler
long-handled wooden
    spoon

INGREDIENTS:

1 medium-size cucumber,
    about 6 inches long
1 small onion
1 small red pepper (or
    green if red is
    unavailable)
2 tablespoons red wine
    vinegar
2 tablespoons plain nonfat
    or low-fat yogurt
1 tablespoon chopped
    fresh dill *or* 1
    teaspoon dried dill
1 tablespoon chopped
    fresh parsley *or* 1
    teaspoon dried
    parsley
1/8 teaspoon black pepper

This salad is low in calories, fat-free, and full of vitamin C from the red pepper. Use a red pepper if you can because red peppers have 10 times more vitamin C and somewhat more vitamin A than green peppers.

DIRECTIONS:

1. Wash the cucumber and peel it. Slice the cucumber into thin circles.

2. Cut the ends off of the onion and peel away the outer skin. Slice the onion into very thin circles (as thin as you can).

3. Cut the red pepper in half lengthwise and remove the stem and seeds. Wash the halves and cut them into small chunks.

4. Combine the vinegar, yogurt, dill, parsley, and black pepper in a medium bowl and stir with a wooden spoon until all of the spices are thoroughly combined. Add the cucumber, onion, and red pepper and toss until the vegetables are evenly coated with the dressing.

Per serving: Calories: 19; Total Fat: less than 1 gram; Saturated Fat: 0 grams; Sodium: 5 milligrams; Cholesterol: 0 milligrams.

PEPPATO SALAD

This salad tastes best when you use summer tomatoes that have been allowed to ripen on the vine.

Serves 5   Intermediate

TOOLS:

fork
cutting board
measuring cup
medium serving bowl
small mixing bowl
small, sharp knife
measuring spoons
long-handled wooden
    spoon

INGREDIENTS:

3 large, ripe tomatoes
1 large green pepper
¼ cup red wine vinegar
2 teaspoons olive oil
½ teaspoon Dijon-style
    mustard
1 tablespoon chopped
    fresh parsley *or* 1
    teaspoon dried
    parsley

"My veggie friends call me Mr. C.
Can you guess why?
Well, if you guessed that I'm rich in vitamin C,
then you're as right as you could be!"

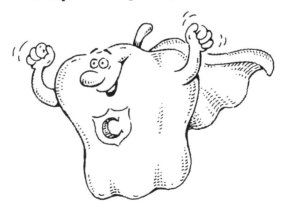

DIRECTIONS:

1. Wash the tomatoes and remove the stem end. Cut the tomatoes into cubes that will easily fit in your mouth.

2. Cut the pepper in half lengthwise and remove the stem and seeds. Wash the halves and cut them into chunks that will easily fit in your mouth.

3. In a small bowl, combine the vinegar, oil, mustard, and parsley. Stir with a fork until combined.

4. Place the tomatoes, pepper, and dressing in a medium serving bowl and toss with a wooden spoon until the dressing is evenly distributed.

Per serving: Calories: 45; Total Fat: 2.5 grams (.6 teaspoons); Saturated Fat: 0.3 grams; Sodium: 16 milligrams; Cholesterol: 0 milligrams.

CORNY BREAD

This recipe is easy to prepare and delicious served with Beans-and-Veggies Chili (page 88).

Serves 12   Intermediate

TOOLS:

measuring cups
egg beater
large mixing bowl
9-inch square pan
toothpick
measuring spoons
long-handled wooden
    spoon
small mixing bowl
hot pad or wire rack
timer

INGREDIENTS:

Vegetable oil spray
1 cup cornmeal
$\frac{1}{2}$ cup all-purpose flour
$\frac{1}{2}$ cup whole-wheat flour
2 teaspoons baking
    powder
1 teaspoon baking soda
$\frac{1}{3}$ cup sugar
$\frac{1}{4}$ teaspoon salt
1 egg
1 egg white
$1\frac{1}{4}$ cups buttermilk
2 tablespoons vegetable
    oil
$\frac{1}{4}$ cup frozen corn

DIRECTIONS:

1. Preheat the oven to 450 degrees and lightly spray a baking pan with vegetable oil spray.

2. Combine the cornmeal, flours, baking powder, baking soda, sugar, and salt in a large bowl. Stir with a wooden spoon until well mixed.

3. Place the egg and egg white in a small bowl. Using an egg beater, whip until they are a light yellow.

4. Add the beaten eggs, buttermilk, and oil to the flour mixture. Mix with the wooden spoon until all of the dry ingredients are wet and evenly combined. Add the corn and stir until the kernels are coated with batter.

5. Pour the batter into the prepared pan. Put your oven mitts on, open the oven door, and place the pan in the middle of the center rack. Set the timer and bake the cornbread for 20 minutes.

6. When the timer goes off, put your oven mitts back on and pull out the rack just enough to be able to insert a toothpick into the center of the bread. If it comes out dry, then the bread is done. If the toothpick still has some wet batter on it, then cook until done.

7. Remove the bread from the oven and place on a wire rack or hot pad to cool.

Per serving: Calories: 123; Total Fat: 3.4 grams (.8 teaspoons); Saturated Fat: 0.5 grams; Sodium: 200 milligrams; Cholesterol: 24 milligrams.

The vitamins and minerals in the foods you eat are invisible, but their hard work to keep your body healthy is very plain to see.

TURKEY BAR-B-Q

This sweet and spicy barbecue served over a crusty roll was a favorite with our recipe tasters.

Serves 6   Master

TOOLS:

measuring cup
cutting board
small, sharp knife
long-handled wooden
    spoon
measuring spoons
large frying pan or electric
    skillet
medium mixing bowl
can opener

INGREDIENTS:

1 small onion
$\frac{1}{2}$ medium-size green
    pepper
$\frac{1}{2}$ cup unsweetened
    pineapple juice
1 pound ground turkey
1 6-ounce can tomato
    paste, no salt added
$\frac{1}{2}$ cup water
2 teaspoons Dijon-style
    mustard (or any spicy
    mustard)
$\frac{1}{2}$ teaspoon garlic powder
6 whole-grain sandwich
    rolls

DIRECTIONS:

1. Slice the ends off of the onion and peel away the outer skin. Chop the onion into small pieces about the size of a pencil eraser.

2. Remove the stem and seeds from the green pepper half. Wash it and chop it into pieces about the same size as the onion. (Store the other half of the pepper in an airtight container in the refrigerator.)

3. Pour the pineapple juice into a frying pan and heat on medium. Add the chopped onion and green pepper. Cook and stir with a wooden spoon over medium heat until the onion gets soft (the color of the onion will change from white to a transparent yellow).

4. Add the ground turkey and turn the heat up to medium-high. Cook and stir until the turkey turns light brown.

5. Mix the tomato paste, water, mustard, and garlic powder in a medium bowl with the wooden spoon. Stir until mixed well. Add to the turkey and stir (about 25 circles). Turn the heat down to low and simmer for 30 minutes.

6. Serve on whole-grain rolls.

Per serving: Calories: 247; Total Fat: 5 grams (1.1 teaspoons); Saturated Fat: 3.7 grams; Sodium: 304 milligrams; Cholesterol: 23 milligrams.

"I have less fat than beef, but I do have fat that I hide in my dark meat and skin."

LEMON CHICKEN

If you love the tangy taste of lemons, you'll flip over this recipe.

Serves 4   Intermediate

TOOLS:

cutting board
timer
measuring cup
9-inch-by-9-inch baking
    dish
small, sharp knife
measuring spoons
paper towels

INGREDIENTS:

2 lemons
4 skinless, boneless
    chicken breast halves
2 cups chicken broth,
    homemade or low-
    sodium canned
1 teaspoon marjoram
1 teaspoon oregano
$\frac{1}{2}$ teaspoon black pepper

Safety Alert! After you touch raw chicken, it is very important to wash your hands and kitchen tools with hot, soapy water. Dangerous bacteria may be living on the chicken.

DIRECTIONS:

1. Preheat the oven to 375 degrees.
2. Wash the lemons and slice them into thin, round circles. Place half of the lemon slices on the bottom of a baking dish.
3. Wash the chicken breasts and pat them dry with paper towels, then lay them on top of the lemon slices in the baking dish.
4. Pour the chicken broth on top of the chicken breasts.
5. Sprinkle the chicken breasts with the marjoram, oregano, and black pepper.
6. Place the remaining lemon slices on top of the chicken.
7. Wash your hands, the cutting board, and the knife with hot, soapy water.
8. Put your oven mitts on, open the oven door, and place the pan in the middle of the center rack. Set the timer and bake the chicken for 40 minutes.

Per serving: Calories: 162; Total Fat: 3.8 grams (.9 teaspoons); Saturated Fat: 1.1 grams; Sodium: 90 milligrams; Cholesterol: 73 milligrams.

SUPER STIR-FRY

When preparing this dish, keep all of the vegetables that you are slicing in separate piles since you will be adding them to the wok at different times.

Serves 4   Master

TOOLS:

cutting board
measuring cup
long-handled wooden
  spoon
wok or large frying pan
small, sharp knife
measuring spoons
garlic press
vegetable peeler
paper towels

INGREDIENTS:

2 garlic cloves
2 large stalks broccoli
3 carrots, about 5 inches
  long
6 to 8 fresh mushrooms
1 medium-size green
  pepper
1 medium-size onion
1 teaspoon peanut oil
1 tablespoon water
1 tablespoon mild or low-
  sodium soy sauce
Firm tofu, cut into small
  cubes to make ¾ cup

DIRECTIONS:

1. Peel the garlic and force it through a garlic press. Set aside. (If you don't have a garlic press, then just chop the garlic into tiny pieces.)

2. Wash the broccoli and cut off the florets.

3. Peel the carrots, cut off the tops and bottoms, and slice the carrots into coin-shaped pieces.

4. Wipe the mushrooms with a damp paper towel and cut off the end part of each stem. Slice the mushrooms into thin pieces to make 1 cup.

5. Cut the green pepper in half lengthwise and remove the stem and seeds. Wash the halves and cut them into small strips (about 1 inch long and ½ inch wide).

6. Cut the ends off the onion and peel the outer skin. Slice the onion into thick disks, then separate into rings.

7. In a wok or frying pan, heat the oil on medium-high heat.

8. Add the garlic and onion and stir with a wooden spoon for 15 seconds.

9. Stir in the broccoli florets, carrots, and green pepper.

10. Add the water. Cover the pan and cook until the vegetables are about half-done, about 6 minutes.

11. Add the soy sauce and stir well with the wooden spoon.

12. Stir in the mushrooms and tofu and cook for another 5 minutes. Serve immediately. Try eating this meal with chopsticks instead of forks!

Per serving: Calories: 116; Total Fat: 3.9 grams (.9 teaspoons); Saturated Fat: 0.5 grams; Sodium: 214 milligrams; Cholesterol: 0 milligrams.

This oriental way to cook is healthy because you use a small amount of fat and cook the vegetables for a short time, which helps preserve their nutrients. The tofu is rich in protein and is a substitute for chicken or beef. Remember to use reduced-sodium soy sauce!

FABULOUS FISH STICKS

Forget those rock-hard sticks in the freezer—try this recipe and do it yourself!

Serves 4   Master

TOOLS:

measuring cup
small mixing bowl
nonstick baking dish
measuring spoons
timer
dinner plate
fork or wire whisk
Ziploc plastic bag
rolling pin
small, sharp knife
cutting board

INGREDIENTS:

1 pound boneless,
    skinless cod
1 egg white
¼ cup skim milk
3 to 4 slices dry bread
½ teaspoon black pepper
1 teaspoon dried parsley
¼ teaspoon paprika
½ lemon, cut into wedges

"Flounder, sole, tuna, or trout,
do the right thing—check them out.
Don't end up a cardiac dude,
bust the fat right out of your food."

DIRECTIONS:

1. Preheat the oven to 475 degrees.

2. Cut the fish into 8 stick-shaped pieces. Try to make them as equal in size as possible.

3. Combine the egg and milk in a small bowl and briskly whip with a fork or wire whisk until foamy (about 15 quick strokes).

4. Place the bread in a plastic bag. Close the bag and crush the bread into fine crumbs by rolling over it with the rolling pin. Measure out 1 cup of crumbs. With your fingers, mix together the bread crumbs, pepper, parsley, and paprika on a dinner plate.

5. Dip the fish into the egg mixture, coat with the crumb mixture, and place the fish in a nonstick baking dish (if using a regular baking dish, lightly grease the bottom with vegetable oil so the fish will not stick during cooking). Repeat this procedure until all the fish is breaded, then squeeze the lemon juice evenly over the fish sticks.

6. Put your oven mitts on, open the oven door, and place the dish in the middle of the center rack. Set the timer and bake the fish sticks for 20 minutes.

7. Serve with your favorite green vegetable and a baked potato.

Per serving: Calories: 201; Total Fat: 2.1 grams (.5 teaspoons); Saturated Fat: 0.5 grams; Sodium: 266 milligrams; Cholesterol: 51 milligrams.

SAUCY SPAGHETTI

This tomato sauce can also be used for pizza or to serve over chicken.

Serves 4   Intermediate

TOOLS:

measuring cups
large frying pan
colander
small, sharp knife
6- or 8-quart pot
measuring spoons
long-handled wooden
    spoon
cutting board
garlic press
tongs
can opener

INGREDIENTS:

1 small onion
2 garlic cloves
1 medium-size green
    pepper
1 tablespoon olive oil
1 6-ounce can tomato
    paste, no salt added
1 cup tomato sauce, no
    salt added
1 teaspoon basil
$\frac{1}{2}$ teaspoon oregano
8 ounces spaghetti (half of
    a 1-pound box)
$\frac{1}{3}$ cup grated Parmesan
    cheese

DIRECTIONS:

1. Slice off the ends of the onion, peel away the outer skin, and chop the onion into pieces about the size of a pencil eraser.

2. Peel the garlic and force it through a garlic press. If there are still large pieces, you may have to chop these by hand. (If you don't have a garlic press, then just chop the garlic into tiny pieces.)

3. Cut the green pepper in half lengthwise and remove the

stem and seeds. Wash the halves and chop them into pieces about the size of a pencil eraser.

4. Put the oil in a frying pan and turn the heat to medium-high. Place the onion, garlic, and green pepper in the frying pan and heat until softened.

5. Add the tomato paste, tomato sauce, basil, and oregano and stir with a wooden spoon. Turn the heat down to low.

6. Let this simmer while you cook the spaghetti in a large pot according to the directions on the box.

7. Place a colander in the sink. When the spaghetti is cooked, drain the water in the colander. Using tongs, place a mound of spaghetti on dinner plates and top with the hot sauce and Parmesan cheese.

Per serving: Calories: 323; Total Fat: 7.4 grams (1.7 teaspoons); Saturated Fat: 2.2 grams; Sodium: 189 milligrams; Cholesterol: 7 milligrams.

Quiz time: What fat-free, low-calorie, bright red food is called a vegetable but is really a fruit loaded with vitamin A and vitamin C?

Answer: Tomato.

SOUTH-OF-THE-BORDER
CASSEROLE

Why not do a little Mexican hat dance while this casserole bakes in the oven?

Serves 4   Master

TOOLS:

measuring cups
small, sharp knife
cutting board
fork
large nonstick frying pan
    (or frying pan lightly
    greased with
    vegetable oil)
9-inch square baking dish
measuring spoons
small mixing bowl
timer
large mixing bowl
2 long-handled wooden
    spoons
wire rack

INGREDIENTS:

1 medium-size onion
1 medium-size green
    pepper
$1/2$ pound ground turkey
1 cup tomato sauce, no
    salt added
1 cup home-cooked or
    frozen corn
1 teaspoon Worcestershire
    sauce
$1^1/2$ teaspoons chili
    powder
1 cup cornmeal
$1/2$ cup all-purpose flour
1 teaspoon baking powder
$1/2$ teaspoon baking soda
3 tablespoons sugar
$3/4$ cup skim milk
1 egg
1 tablespoon vegetable oil
2 tablespoons canned,
    chopped green
    chilies

"Hey, amigo, want some fat-saving advice about Mexican foods? Stick to chicken or beans served with soft (not fried) tortillas, and avoid sour cream topping and gobs of cheese."

DIRECTIONS:

1. Preheat the oven to 350 degrees.

2. Slice the ends off of the onion, peel away the outer skin, and chop the onion into small pieces.

3. Slice the green pepper in half lengthwise and remove the stem and seeds. Wash the halves and chop them into pieces the same size as the onion.

4. Place the onion, green pepper, and turkey in a frying pan and heat on medium-high for 10 minutes, stirring continuously with a wooden spoon.

5. Turn off the heat and add the tomato sauce, corn, Worcestershire sauce, and chili powder to the mixture. Stir with the wooden spoon (about 10 circles). Place this mixture in a baking dish and smooth it out with the wooden spoon. Set this aside for now.

6. In a large mixing bowl, combine the cornmeal, flour, baking powder, baking soda, and sugar. Stir with a clean wooden spoon (about 8 circles).

7. In a small mixing bowl, combine the milk, egg, and oil. Whip with a fork until the yellow of the egg is thoroughly combined and the mixture is a light yellow. Stir in the green chilies.

8. Add the egg mixture to the dry ingredients in the large bowl. Quickly mix with the wooden spoon until combined (about 20 circles).

9. Immediately spoon the cornmeal mixture around the edges of the turkey filling in the baking dish.

10. Put on your oven mitts, open the oven door, and place the baking dish in the middle of the center rack. Set the timer for 30 minutes.

11. When the timer goes off, put your oven mitts back on and place the baking pan on a wire rack to cool for about 5 to 7 minutes before serving.

Per serving: Calories: 452; Total Fat: 9 grams (2.1 teaspoons); Saturated Fat: 4.0 grams; Sodium: 329 milligrams; Cholesterol: 89 milligrams.

OPEN SESAME CHICKEN

Crispy and juicy chicken nuggets with a dynamite taste.

Serves 5   Master

TOOLS:

Ziploc plastic bag
small, sharp knife
measuring cups
2 small mixing bowls
paper towels
fork
rolling pin or mallet
cutting board
timer
measuring spoons
spoon
nonstick cookie sheet

INGREDIENTS:

Vegetable oil spray
1 pound boneless,
    skinless chicken
    breasts
2 cups Spoon Size
    Shredded Wheat
    cereal
$\frac{1}{4}$ cup sesame seeds
1 tablespoon chopped
    fresh parsley *or* 1
    teaspoon dried
    parsley
$\frac{1}{8}$ teaspoon garlic powder
$\frac{1}{8}$ teaspoon powdered
    ginger
1 tablespoon olive oil
1 tablespoon lemon juice
1 egg white

Sauce:

1 cup plain nonfat or low-
    fat yogurt
1 tablespoon honey
$1\frac{1}{2}$ teaspoons Dijon-style
    mustard
1 teaspoon reduced-
    sodium soy sauce

This recipe has less than 2 teaspoons of fat per serving. Compare that to the 4 teaspoons of fat in a serving of fast-food chicken nuggets with mustard sauce. What a fat-saver.

DIRECTIONS:

1. Preheat the oven to 350 degrees. Coat a cookie sheet by spraying lightly with vegetable oil spray.

2. Wash the chicken breasts and pat them dry with paper towels.

3. Place the cereal in a plastic bag and crush it by rolling over it with a rolling pin or pounding it with a mallet.

4. Place the sesame seeds, parsley, garlic powder, and ginger in the bag with the crushed cereal. Close the bag and shake to mix well.

5. Place the olive oil, lemon juice, and egg white in a small bowl. Using a fork, whip them until they are foamy (about 30 quick strokes).

6. Cut the chicken into one-inch-square pieces. Dip the chicken pieces into the oil and egg mixture. Let the excess drip off and then place the chicken pieces in the plastic bag. Seal the bag and shake until they are coated with the cereal mix. Repeat until all the pieces are coated.

7. Place the coated chicken on the cookie sheet, set the timer, and bake the chicken for 15 minutes. Wash your hands, the knife, and the cutting board with hot, soapy water.

8. While the chicken is baking, place the yogurt, honey, mustard, and soy sauce in a small mixing bowl and mix with a spoon until thoroughly combined.

9. Serve the chicken nuggets with the sauce.

Per serving: Calories: 269; Total Fat: 7.9 grams (1.8 teaspoons); Saturated Fat: 1.3 grams; Sodium: 198 milligrams; Cholesterol: 55 milligrams.

BEANS-AND-VEGGIES CHILI

A steaming bowl of chili is just what you need to get your motor into high gear.

Serves 4   Master

TOOLS:

can opener
measuring cups
small, sharp knife
cutting board
large, heavy pot
measuring spoons
long-handled wooden
    spoon

INGREDIENTS:

2 medium-size onions
1 garlic clove
1 medium-size green pepper
1 small celery stalk
1 tablespoon olive oil or
    vegetable oil
1 medium-size tomato
1 cup tomato puree, no salt
    added
1 cup water
1 6-ounce can tomato paste,
    no salt added
2 tablespoons brown sugar
1 tablespoon oregano
1½ teaspoons chili powder
    (you can use more if
    you like it hot)
2 teaspoons ground cumin
¼ teaspoon allspice
1½ cups home-cooked or
    canned kidney beans
    (drained and rinsed)
1½ cups home-cooked or
    canned black beans
    (drained and rinsed)
½ cup home cooked or
    frozen corn

"You may have heard of chili con carne,
which is Spanish for chili with meat. This chili is
made without 'carne,' which reduces
the fat and cholesterol
and keeps me out of the pot!"

DIRECTIONS:

1. Cut the ends off of the onions, peel them, and chop them coarsely to fill 1 cup. The pieces should be about the size of a raisin.

2. Peel the garlic and chop it very fine.

3. Cut the green pepper in half lengthwise and remove the stem and seeds. Wash it and chop it into small pieces.

4. Wash the celery and cut off the leafy top. Chop the celery into small pieces to fill ⅓ cup.

5. In a large, heavy pot, heat the oil on medium (the oil should not sizzle or turn brown). Add the chopped vegetables and heat until the onion turns a pale yellow and the green pepper becomes soft.

6. Wash the tomato and remove the stem end. Chop the tomato into small chunks. Add the tomato, tomato puree, water, and tomato paste to the pot. Stir with the spoon.

7. Add the brown sugar, oregano, chili powder, cumin, all-spice, and beans and stir once or twice. Bring the mixture to a boil (bubbles will appear at the surface). After it boils, turn down the heat to low, cover the pot, and cook for 25 minutes.

8. After cooking for 25 minutes on low heat, add the corn. Stir with the wooden spoon to combine everything (about 6 circles). Heat for another 5 minutes on low. Using pot holders and both hands, remove the chili from the stove and serve in bowls. This recipe tastes great with Corny Bread (see page 70).

Per serving: Calories: 357; Total Fat: 5.4 grams (1.2 teaspoons); Saturated Fat: 0.7 grams; Sodium: 72 milligrams; Cholesterol: 0 milligrams. (Note: Nutritional analysis based on home-cooked beans.)

DEEP-SEA CASSEROLE

A tuna-noodle casserole that will tempt your tastebuds.

Serves 4   Intermediate

TOOLS:

large mixing bowl
can opener
measuring spoons
6- or 8-quart pot
colander
small, sharp knife
aluminum foil
blender or food processor
measuring cups
long-handled wooden
    spoon
2-quart baking dish
cutting board
wire rack
timer
paper towels

INGREDIENTS:

Vegetable oil spray
6 ounces seashell pasta (2
    cups)
1 6$\frac{1}{2}$-ounce can tuna,
    packed in water
5 to 6 medium-size fresh
    mushrooms
1 small green pepper
2 scallions (green onions)
$\frac{1}{2}$ cup 1 percent low-fat
    cottage cheese
$\frac{1}{4}$ cup part-skim ricotta
    cheese
$\frac{1}{2}$ cup skim milk
2 tablespoons olive oil
2 tablespoons chopped
    fresh parsley or 2
    teaspoons dried
    parsley
$\frac{1}{2}$ teaspoon dried oregano
$\frac{1}{4}$ teaspoon dried basil
$\frac{1}{4}$ teaspoon black pepper

"Do you think I'm fatten-
ing? Forget the rumors—
I'm not. The fact is, I am a
healthy food high in starch
and low in fat."

DIRECTIONS:

1. Preheat the oven to 400 degrees and spray a baking dish with a light coat of vegetable oil spray.

2. Boil the pasta in a large pot according to the directions on the package.

3. While the pasta is boiling, open the can of tuna. Place the tuna in a colander and wash it with water for about 1 minute to remove most of the salt. Place the tuna in a large mixing bowl and rinse the colander because you will use it later to drain the pasta.

4. Wipe the mushrooms with a damp paper towel and cut off the end part of each stem. Slice the mushrooms into thin pieces and place them in the large bowl.

5. Cut the green pepper in half lengthwise and remove the stem and seeds. Wash the halves, cut them into small pieces, and place them in the large bowl.

6. Wash the scallions, cut them into small pieces (use both the white bulbs and the green tops), and place them in the large bowl.

7. In a blender or food processor, combine the cottage cheese, ricotta cheese, milk, olive oil, parsley, oregano, basil, and black pepper. Blend until the seasonings are combined and the mixture looks smooth (about 2 minutes).

8. Add the cooked, drained pasta and the cheese sauce to the large mixing bowl. Stir all of the ingredients using a wooden spoon until the sauce evenly coats the pasta.

9. Place the casserole ingredients into the prepared baking dish. Smooth off the top using the wooden spoon and cover with aluminum foil. Put your oven mitts on, open the oven door, and place the baking dish in the middle of the center rack. Set the timer and bake the casserole for 10 minutes. Remove the aluminum foil (use your oven mitts!), reset the timer, and bake the casserole for another 10 minutes. Let cool on a wire rack for 10 minutes, then serve.

Per serving: Calories: 339; Total Fat: 9.9 grams (2.2 teaspoons); Saturated Fat: 2.1 grams; Sodium: 195 milligrams; Cholesterol: 30 milligrams. (Note: Nutritional analysis based on rinsed tuna.)

DESSERTS AND SNACKS

Apple Crisp
Rice Pudding
Berry Pops
Fruit Kabobs
Hummus Is Among Us
Cottage Cheese Dip
Chips for Dips
Roll-Ups
Cinnamon Stars
Yummy Crumby Blueberry Cake
Sunshine Pie

APPLE CRISP

The reward for slicing the apples is the warm, delicious taste of this dessert.

Serves 6   Intermediate

TOOLS:

cutting board
measuring cups
large mixing bowl
1-quart pan
small, sharp knife
measuring spoons
wire rack
timer
long-handled wooden
    spoon
8-inch square baking dish
    or pan

INGREDIENTS:

Apple mixture:
1 teaspoon vegetable oil
7 apples
2 tablespoons lemon
    juice, bottled or fresh
1 tablespoon whole-wheat
    flour
1½ teaspoons cinnamon

Topping:
3 tablespoons margarine
¼ cup whole-wheat flour
1 cup old-fashioned oats
½ teaspoon cinnamon
¼ cup brown sugar

DIRECTIONS:

1. Preheat the oven to 375 degrees.

2. Pour the oil into a baking dish and spread it around with your fingers or with a napkin. Set the dish aside.

3. To make the apple mixture, wash the apples and remove the stems. Slice each apple into quarters and remove the core and seeds. Cut the apples into thin slices, about 4 to 5 slices for each quarter.

4. In a large bowl, combine the apples, lemon juice, flour, and cinnamon. Using a wooden spoon, stir and toss this mixture for about 2 minutes. When this is thoroughly mixed, place it in the prepared baking dish. Rinse and dry the wooden spoon.

5. To make the topping, melt the margarine in a pan over low heat. Remove from the heat and add the flour, oats, cinnamon, and brown sugar. Using the wooden spoon, stir to combine (about 20 circles).

6. Sprinkle the oat mixture over the apples in the baking dish.

7. Put your oven mitts on, open the oven door, and place the baking dish in the middle of the center rack. Set your timer for 50 minutes. Let the apple crisp cool on a wire rack for about 15 minutes before serving.

Per serving: Calories: 257; Total Fat: 7.3 grams (1.7 teaspoons); Saturated Fat: 1.4 grams; Sodium: 71 milligrams; Cholesterol: 0 milligrams.

Cut the fat! This apple crisp recipe uses less margarine than traditional recipes for this dessert.

RICE PUDDING

This rice pudding has a slightly nutty flavor because of the brown rice.

Serves 8   Master

TOOLS:

1½-quart pan with lid
measuring spoons
wire rack
medium mixing bowl
measuring cups
long-handled wooden
    spoon
egg beater
can opener

INGREDIENTS:

1¾ cups water
½ cup uncooked brown
    rice
1½ cups 1 percent low-fat
    milk
½ cup canned evaporated
    skim milk
1 egg
2 egg whites
¼ cup sugar
1 teaspoon vanilla extract
⅓ cup raisins
½ teaspoon cinnamon

Brown rice has more dietary fiber than white rice because the white loses the husk, bran, and germ during processing.

DIRECTIONS:

1. Put the water and rice in a pan and bring to a boil (when the water bubbles very fast). Cover the pan tightly, reduce the heat to low, and cook for about 40 minutes. Watch carefully in the beginning so that it doesn't boil over and at the end so that it doesn't become too dry and burn.

2. Whip the milks, egg, egg whites, sugar, and vanilla in a medium bowl with an egg beater until well mixed (about 50 quick strokes).

3. Add this mixture to the cooked rice. Bring to a boil again, stirring frequently with a wooden spoon. When it starts to bubble, add the raisins and turn the heat down to low so the pudding will simmer. Cook for another 10 minutes— stirring all the time.

4. Using pot holders and both hands, remove the pan from the heat and set it on a wire rack to cool. Sprinkle the cinnamon on the top. Serve the pudding warm or chilled.

Per serving: Calories: 127; Total Fat: 1.6 grams (.4 teaspoons); Saturated Fat: 0.6 grams; Sodium: 64 milligrams; Cholesterol: 37 milligrams.

BERRY POPS

Fruit-sicles are a great treat on a hot summer day.

Serves 12   Intermediate

TOOLS:

measuring cups
1-quart pan
hot pad
blender or food processor
12 wooden sticks
    (available at most
    supermarkets and
    craft stores)
measuring spoon
small, sharp knife
long-handled wooden
    spoon
12 4-ounce paper cups
cookie sheet
aluminum foil

INGREDIENTS:

1/2 cup berry juice blend,
    such as cranberry-
    raspberry,
    boysenberry, apple-
    raspberry
1 tablespoon (1 envelope)
    unflavored gelatin
2 cups nonfat or low-fat
    vanilla yogurt
1 1/2 cups frozen,
    unsweetened berries
    (blueberries,
    strawberries,
    raspberries, or
    blackberries)

DIRECTIONS:

1. Place the juice in a pan and sprinkle the gelatin over it. Cook over low heat, stirring constantly with a wooden spoon until the gelatin crystals dissolve and disappear. Using a pot holder and both hands, remove the pan from the heat and place on a hot pad.

2. In a blender or food processor, mix the yogurt, berries, and warm gelatin mixture. Blend until smooth (about 2 minutes).

3. Place the paper cups on a cookie sheet (one that will fit in the freezer). Fill the cups with the blended mixture and place a sheet of aluminum foil over the tops of the cups.

4. Insert the stick for each pop by making a slit in the foil with a knife over the center of each cup and placing the stick into the cup. The aluminum foil will help keep the stick in place.

5. Place the tray in the freezer and freeze until hard.

6. Remove the pops from the cups by peeling away the paper.

Per berry pop: Calories: 42; Total Fat: less than 1 gram; Saturated Fat: 0.1 gram; Sodium: 26 milligrams; Cholesterol: 0 milligrams.

Homemade is better! Most ice pops are made from water, sugar, artificial colors, and artificial flavors. These pops are made with real fruit.

FRUIT KABOBS

A fun recipe to make with family or friends!

Serves 6   Rookie

TOOLS:

measuring cups
cutting board
small mixing bowl
small serrated knife
measuring spoon
sieve
butter knife
small spoon
6 wooden skewers
can opener

INGREDIENTS:

1 cup pineapple chunks,
    packed in juice
$1/4$ cup orange juice
$1/2$ teaspoon cinnamon
2 bananas, about 6 inches
    long
12 fresh strawberries
18 seedless green grapes

Fruits are rich in naturally occurring sugar, so they taste sweet like candy, but fruits have vitamins, minerals, and fiber, too!

DIRECTIONS:

1. Open the can of pineapple and drain the liquid through a sieve into a small mixing bowl. Set the pineapple chunks aside. Add the orange juice and cinnamon to the liquid and mix with a small spoon until combined.

2. Peel the bananas and cut each banana into 6 pieces with a butter knife.

3. Put the banana pieces into the bowl with the juice and toss until all of the pieces are coated. Set aside.

4. Wash the strawberries and grapes. Carefully remove the stems from the strawberries using a serrated knife.

5. Place the pineapple chunks, banana chunks, green grapes, and strawberries within easy reach. Build the kabobs by piercing alternating fruits with the wooden skewers. Each skewer will have 2 banana chunks, 3 grapes, 3 or 4 pineapple chunks, and 2 strawberries.

Per kabob: Calories: 106; Total Fat: less than 1 gram; Saturated Fat: 0.1 grams; Sodium: 2 milligrams; Cholesterol: 0 milligrams.

HUMMUS IS AMONG US

What is hummus? Well, it is a Middle Eastern food made from chick-peas and sesame paste that can be eaten as a dip, a sandwich spread, or a filling for pita bread!

Serves 8   Intermediate

TOOLS:

cutting board
hot pad
measuring cups
small frying pan
small bowl
serving bowl
small, sharp knife
measuring spoon
sieve
long-handled wooden
    spoon
blender or food processor
can opener

INGREDIENTS:

1 garlic clove
1 tablespoon olive oil
1 medium-size lemon
2 sprigs fresh parsley
    (enough for 1
    tablespoon chopped)
2 cups home-cooked or
    canned chick-peas
    (also called garbanzo
    beans)
¼ cup tahini (sesame
    seed paste)

For dipping:
2 whole-wheat pita
    pockets, cut into
    wedges, or 20 raw
    carrot sticks, celery
    sticks, broccoli
    florets, or other
    vegetables

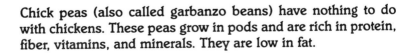

Chick peas (also called garbanzo beans) have nothing to do with chickens. These peas grow in pods and are rich in protein, fiber, vitamins, and minerals. They are low in fat.

104

DIRECTIONS:

1. Peel and very finely chop the garlic.

2. Place the oil in a small frying pan and turn the heat to medium. Add the garlic and cook for 1 or 2 minutes, stirring with a wooden spoon. Watch this carefully and turn the heat down to low if the garlic starts to brown around the edges. Using pot holders and both hands, remove the pan from the heat and set aside on a hot pad.

3. Cut the lemon in half and squeeze it into a small bowl until all of the juice is drained. Remove any seeds.

4. Cut the parsley into small pieces, but don't chop it, since the blender will do that job.

5. If using canned chick-peas, open the can, drain the liquid into a sieve, and rinse the chick-peas with water.

6. In a blender or food processor, combine the chick-peas, tahini, garlic, lemon juice, and parsley. Puree until it is smooth, about 5 minutes.

7. Transfer the hummus to a serving bowl. Use a wooden spoon to scrape the sides of the blender or processor.

8. Eat immediately with pita bread or fresh vegetable sticks, or cover and store in the refrigerator.

Per 1/3-cup serving: Calories: 170; Total Fat: 7.3 grams (1.6 teaspoons); Saturated Fat: 1.1 grams; Sodium: 107 milligrams; Cholesterol: 0 milligrams. (Note: Nutritional analysis based on home-cooked chick-peas.)

COTTAGE CHEESE DIP

Cut up some broccoli, cauliflower, and other fresh vegetables and have a "dipping" party with your family or friends.

Serves 6   Rookie

TOOLS:

measuring cup
medium mixing bowl
measuring spoons
blender or food processor
aluminum foil

INGREDIENTS:

1 12-ounce carton low-fat
    (1 percent) cottage
    cheese
$\frac{1}{2}$ cup plain nonfat or
    low-fat yogurt
$1\frac{1}{2}$ teaspoons chopped
    fresh dill *or* $\frac{1}{2}$
    teaspoon dried dill
$\frac{1}{2}$ teaspoon onion powder
$\frac{1}{4}$ teaspoon garlic powder
$\frac{1}{8}$ teaspoon black pepper

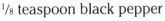

When you and your friends have a "snack attack," get dipping
with this low-fat recipe that's packed with protein and calcium.

DIRECTIONS:

1. Place all the ingredients in a blender or food processor. Blend until smooth, about 3 minutes.

2. Pour the mixture into a medium bowl and cover with aluminum foil. Place in the refrigerator and chill before serving.

Per ⅓-cup serving: Calories: 52; Total Fat: less than 1 gram; Saturated Fat: 0.4 grams; Sodium: 244 milligrams; Cholesterol: 3 milligrams. (Note: You can cut the sodium of this recipe almost in half by using ¾ cup of dry-curd cottage cheese mixed with ¾ cup of 1 percent cottage cheese.)

CHIPS FOR DIPS

Yippee! A tortilla chip that is not loaded with fat.

Serves 4   Intermediate

TOOLS:

large serrated knife
cutting board
dish towel
cookie sheet
timer
measuring spoon

INGREDIENTS:

4 corn tortillas
Vegetable oil spray
$\frac{1}{8}$ teaspoon cayenne
     pepper (if desired)

These chips have about half the fat of the tortilla chips you buy in the store.

DIRECTIONS:

1. Preheat the oven to 350 degrees.

2. Place the tortillas in a stack (one stacked evenly on top of the other) on the cutting board. Using a large serrated knife, cut the tortillas into 8 pie-shaped pieces. To do this, cut the stack in half. Then cut each half through the middle the short way. This will leave you with 4 large pie-shaped stacks. Cut each pie-shaped stack in half to make 2 pie-shaped stacks. After cutting each stack in half, you will have a total of 8 pie-shaped stacks.

3. Place tortilla wedges on a cookie sheet so that they do not overlap (use 2 cookie sheets and bake in batches if necessary).

4. Lightly spray both sides of the tortillas with an even coat of vegetable oil spray. Sprinkle them with the pepper if you'd like them spicy. (But be careful—cayenne pepper is *very* hot!)

5. Put your oven mitts on, open the oven door, and place the cookie sheet in the middle of the center rack. Set the timer and bake the chips for 15 minutes.

6. While they are baking, cover the table with a clean dish towel.

7. Put your oven mitts back on and remove the chips from the oven. Dump the chips onto the dish towel to cool, then serve with Cottage Cheese Dip (page 106) or your favorite salsa.

Per serving: Calories: 65; Total Fat: 1.5 grams (.3 teaspoons); Saturated Fat: 1.7 grams; Sodium: 132 milligrams; Cholesterol: 0 milligrams.

ROLL-UPS

Crisp rolls that will satisfy your craving for something sweet.

Makes 8 rolls   Rookie

TOOLS:

rolling pin
measuring cup
cutting board
nonstick cookie sheet
butter knife
measuring spoons
timer
small plastic bag
large serrated knife

INGREDIENTS:

8 slices whole-grain bread
½ cup fruit spread, any
    flavor (this is like jam
    but it is made from
    100 percent fruit; you
    can usually find it in
    the supermarket aisle
    with the jellies and
    jams, but if it is
    unavailable in your
    area, then substitute
    apple butter)
2 tablespoons walnuts
1 teaspoon cinnamon

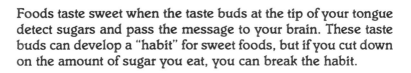

Foods taste sweet when the taste buds at the tip of your tongue detect sugars and pass the message to your brain. These taste buds can develop a "habit" for sweet foods, but if you cut down on the amount of sugar you eat, you can break the habit.

DIRECTIONS:

1. Preheat the oven to 300 degrees.

2. With a large serrated knife, cut the crusts from the bread (nibble while you cook!) and lay the slices flat on your work area. Flatten the bread by rolling the rolling pin several times over each slice (use a little muscle).

3. With a butter knife, spread 1 tablespoon of fruit spread on each of the bread slices.

4. Place the walnuts in a plastic bag. Place the bag on a cutting board. Roll the rolling pin over the bag until the walnuts are crushed.

5. Sprinkle the cinnamon and the crushed walnuts on top of the jam.

6. Roll-up the bread and place seam side down on a non-stick cookie sheet. (If using a regular cookie sheet, grease it lightly by spraying with vegetable oil spray.)

7. Put your oven mitts on, open the oven door, and place the pan in the middle of the center rack. Set the timer for 20 minutes. Cool the roll-ups to room temperature before eating.

Per roll-up: Calories: 122; Total Fat: 2.2 grams (.5 teaspoons); Saturated Fat: 0.5 grams; Sodium: 180 milligrams; Cholesterol: 0 milligrams.

CINNAMON STARS

You will have as much fun making this snack as you will have eating it.

Serves 2   Rookie

TOOLS:

cutting board
timer
butter knife
cookie sheet
measuring spoon
hot pad
star-shaped cookie cutter

INGREDIENTS:

2 slices oatmeal or whole-
    wheat bread
2 teaspoons light cream
    cheese
Cinnamon

DIRECTIONS:

1. Place the bread on the cutting board and cut star shapes from the center of the bread slices. You can nibble on the crusts while you finish the recipe.

2. Place the stars on a cookie sheet, then put your oven mitts on and place the pan under the broiler of an oven. Turn the broiler on, set the timer, and cook the stars for 3 minutes or until browned.

3. Put your oven mitts back on and remove the pan from the oven. Place the pan on a hot pad and spread the cream cheese with a butter knife on one side of the stars.

4. Sprinkle cinnamon over the cream cheese.

Per star: Calories: 78; Total Fat: 1.8 grams (.4 teaspoons); Saturated Fat: 0.7 grams; Sodium: 151 milligrams; Cholesterol: 3 milligrams.

YUMMY CRUMBY
BLUEBERRY CAKE

A moist blueberry cake with crumb topping.

Serves 8   Intermediate

TOOLS:

small mixing bowl
large mixing bowl
electric mixer or egg
    beater
timer
measuring cups
9-inch round cake pan
medium mixing bowl
long-handled wooden
    spoon
butter knife
wire rack
measuring spoons
toothpick

**"What?! You've baked a cake
using about ½ cup of sugar.
Most cake recipes use at
least twice that amount!"**

INGREDIENTS:

Vegetable oil spray

Topping:
²/₃ cup rolled oats
¼ cup all-purpose flour
¼ cup brown sugar
1 tablespoon wheat germ
1 tablespoon apple juice
1 tablespoon softened
    margarine
½ teaspoon nutmeg
½ teaspoon cinnamon

Cake:
1 cup all-purpose flour
½ cup whole-wheat flour
⅓ cup sugar
1½ teaspoons baking
    powder
½ teaspoon baking soda
½ cup plain low-fat yogurt
¼ cup skim milk
1 egg
2 egg whites
2 tablespoons vegetable oil
2 teaspoons vanilla extract
1½ cups blueberries,
    fresh or frozen

DIRECTIONS:

1. Preheat the oven to 350 degrees. Lightly grease a cake pan by spraying with vegetable oil spray.

2. To make the topping, place all of the ingredients in a small bowl. Mix the ingredients with your fingers until they look crumbly. Set the topping mixture aside.

3. To make the cake, combine the flours, sugar, baking powder, and baking soda in a large bowl. Stir these dry ingredients together with a wooden spoon (about 10 to 12 circles).

4. In a medium bowl, combine the yogurt, milk, egg, egg whites, oil, and vanilla. Beat the mixture with an electric mixer set on low for 1 to 2 minutes, or beat by hand with an egg beater until all of the ingredients are well mixed.

5. Add the egg mixture to the flour mixture. With the electric mixer set on medium, beat for about 4 minutes, or combine by hand with the wooden spoon until everything is mixed.

6. Add the blueberries to the batter. Stir with the wooden spoon very carefully so you do not mash the blueberries.

7. Pour the cake batter into the prepared cake pan, then use a butter knife to spread the batter evenly.

8. Sprinkle the topping over the cake batter, covering the top of the batter completely with the crumbs.

9. Put your oven mitts on, open the oven door, and place the cake in the middle of the center rack. Set the timer for 40 minutes. When the timer goes off, check the cake by sticking a toothpick into the center. If it comes out clean or with dry crumbs, then the cake is done. If the

toothpick comes out with wet cake batter, then bake the cake for another 5 minutes.

10. Put your oven mitts back on and place the cake on a wire rack to cool.

Per serving: Calories: 220; Total Fat: 6.8 grams (1.6 teaspoons); Saturated Fat: 1.1 grams; Sodium: 152 milligrams; Cholesterol: 35 milligrams.

SUNSHINE PIE

This dessert uses yogurt cheese, which must be made a day in advance—so plan ahead.

Serves 8   Master

TOOLS:

measuring cups
large and medium mixing
    bowls
can opener
9-inch pie dish
timer
sieve
measuring spoons
wire rack
long-handled wooden
    spoon
blender or food processor
cheesecloth
wire whisk

INGREDIENTS:

16 ounces low-fat vanilla
    yogurt (without
    gelatin)
3/4 cup graham cracker
    crumbs
2 tablespoons softened or
    liquid margarine
1 egg
2 egg whites
1 cup 1 percent low-fat
    cottage cheese
1 tablespoon all-purpose
    flour
1 teaspoon fresh or
    bottled lemon juice
1/4 cup honey
1 cup juice-packed
    pineapple bits,
    drained and liquid
    discarded
1 cup mandarin oranges
    in light syrup, drained
    and liquid discarded

"We replace the high-fat cream cheese
and sour cream in 'real' cheesecake
to help you make a 'heart-happy' dessert."

DIRECTIONS:

1. The day before you make this dessert, make the yogurt cheese. Place a piece of cheesecloth inside a sieve and place the sieve over a medium bowl. Spoon the yogurt into the cheesecloth. Place in the refrigerator overnight. The next day discard the whey (the liquid in the bowl) and use the soft cheese for the recipe.

2. Preheat the oven to 325 degrees.

3. In an ungreased pie dish, combine the graham cracker crumbs and the margarine. Press down on the crumbs with your fingers to form a flat crust against the bottom and the sides, then place the dish in the freezer.

4. In a blender or food processor, combine the egg, egg whites, cottage cheese, flour, lemon juice, and honey and puree until smooth.

5. Pour the cottage cheese mixture into a large bowl (use a wooden spoon to scrape the sides). Add the yogurt cheese and *gently* mix with a wire whisk until thoroughly combined.

6. Remove the crust from the freezer. Pour the cheese mixture into the crust (use the wooden spoon to scrape the sides).

7. Put your oven mitts on, open the oven door, and place the pie dish in the middle of the center rack. Set the timer and bake the pie for 35 minutes.

8. Put your oven mitts back on and place the baking dish on a wire rack to cool.

9. Decorate the top of the pie with the pineapple and oranges. Make a smiling face using 2 orange segments for the eyes and pineapple tidbits for the nose and mouth. Line the rim of the pie with the remaining fruit.

10. Refrigerate until chilled and serve.

Per serving: Calories: 197; Total Fat: 5.1 grams (1.2 teaspoons); Saturated Fat: 1.4 grams; Sodium: 253 milligrams; Cholesterol: 37 milligrams.

BEVERAGES

Honey of a Cow
Orange Cooler
Lime Quencher
Hot Spiced Cider
Fruit Smoothies

HONEY OF A COW

A warm milk drink to relax you when homework is done.

Serves 2   Rookie

TOOLS:

measuring cup
1-quart pan
measuring spoons
long-handled wooden spoon

INGREDIENTS:

2 cups low-fat (1 percent)
    milk
2 teaspoons honey
⅛ teaspoon nutmeg

What has two eyes and lives inside a milk carton?

Answer: Riboflavin, a vitamin that helps the body to produce energy from the foods we eat. It also helps in the growth and repair of body tissue.

DIRECTIONS:

1. Pour the milk into a pan and heat the milk on low, but don't let it come to a boil (bubble).

2. Add the honey and stir with a wooden spoon.

3. Place 2 mugs on the kitchen counter, close to the stove. With your oven mitts on, remove the pan from the stove and carefully pour the warmed milk into the mugs. Sprinkle with a little bit of the nutmeg.

Per serving: Calories: 122; Total Fat: 3.1 grams (.7 teaspoons); Saturated Fat: 1.6 grams; Sodium: 123 milligrams; Cholesterol: 10 milligrams.

ORANGE COOLER

Sparkling orange juice.

Serves 2   Rookie

TOOLS:

large pitcher
long-handled wooden
    spoon
measuring cups
measuring spoon

INGREDIENTS:

2 cups unsweetened
    orange juice
1 tablespoon lemon juice,
    bottled or fresh
1 cup seltzer water

"Orange Cooler is bubbly, zippy, refreshing, and full of vitamin C because of my naturally sweet juice. So who needs soda pop?"

DIRECTIONS:

1. Pour all of the ingredients into a pitcher and stir well with a wooden spoon.

2. Serve immediately in tall glasses.

Per serving: Calories: 112; Total Fat: 0 grams; Saturated Fat: 0 grams; Sodium: 7 milligrams; Cholesterol: 0 milligrams.

LIME QUENCHER

Tangy and thirst quenching.

Serves 5   Rookie

TOOLS:

large pitcher
measuring cups
small, sharp knife
long-handled wooden
    spoon
cutting board
can opener

INGREDIENTS:

³/₄ cup (6 ounces) frozen
    pineapple juice
    concentrate
1 lime
¹/₂ cup lime juice, bottled
    or fresh
1¹/₂ cups water
1¹/₂ cups seltzer water

"Did'ya ever hear of sailors called 'limeys'?
In the eighteenth century, sailors
took crates of limes on long voyages
to prevent scurvy, a disease that
is caused by a lack of vitamin C.
You've probably guessed that
limes have a lot of vitamin C."

124

DIRECTIONS:

1. Hold the can of frozen juice under warm water for a few minutes to soften.

2. Slice the tips off of the lime. Cut the lime into five circular slices. Cut each slice once from the center of the lime out to the rind (this will be called the pinwheel cut) and set aside.

3. Combine the pineapple juice concentrate, lime juice, water, and seltzer in a pitcher and stir with a wooden spoon until the frozen juice dissolves.

4. Pour the beverage into glasses with ice. Place one of the lime slices on each drink by sliding the pinwheel cut over the edge of the glass.

Per 7-ounce serving: Calories: 119; Total Fat: less than 1 gram; Saturated Fat: 0 grams; Sodium: 3 milligrams; Cholesterol: 0 milligrams.

HOT SPICED CIDER

Let this recipe warm you up after a day in the cool autumn breeze.

Serves 2   Intermediate

TOOLS:

measuring cups
sieve
1-quart pan with lid
small, sharp knife
cutting board

INGREDIENTS:

1 small orange *or* ½ large
   orange, any variety
2 cups apple juice or
   cider, unsweetened
3 whole cloves
1 cinnamon stick

Where do the spices cinnamon and cloves come from?

Answer: Cinnamon comes from the bark of special laurel trees, and cloves are the dried unopened flower buds of a large, tropical evergreen tree.

DIRECTIONS:

1. Cut the unpeeled orange into 6 wedges.

2. Combine the orange wedges, apple juice, cloves, and cinnamon stick in a pan.

3. Place the pan over medium-high heat. Bring to a boil (bubble). When it boils, reduce the heat to low. Cover the pan and let the mixture simmer for 15 minutes.

4. Using pot holders and both hands, remove the pan from the heat. Pour the mixture through a sieve (to remove the spices and orange wedges) into mugs. Drink while still warm.

Per serving: Calories: 122; Fat: less than 1 gram; Saturated Fat: 0 grams; Sodium: 7 milligrams; Cholesterol: 0 milligrams.

FRUIT SMOOTHIES

A smoothie is a cool, creamy, fruity drink that is made by blending milk and yogurt with fruit. If you want a frosty cold drink, just add a little ice. The next six recipes are for different-flavored smoothies. Enjoy!

Each recipe serves 2

Mmmmmm! These taste sweet and smooth, and they have loads less fat and cholesterol than a regular ice-cream shake.

GOLDEN SMOOTHIE

Rookie

TOOLS:

measuring spoons
long-handled wooden
    spoon
blender or food processor
cutting board and small,
    sharp knife (for
    Banana Smoothie and
    Mixed-Fruit
    Smoothie)
can opener (for Apricot
    Smoothie and Mixed-
    Fruit Smoothie)
measuring cups

INGREDIENTS:

$1/3$ cup frozen orange juice
    concentrate
$3/4$ cup skim milk
$3/4$ cup nonfat or low-fat
    vanilla yogurt
$1/2$ teaspoon vanilla extract
1 cup ice cubes (optional)

DIRECTIONS:

1. Place the orange juice concentrate, milk, yogurt, vanilla, and ice in a blender or food processor and mix until smooth. Serve immediately in tall glasses.

Per serving: Calories: 150; Total Fat: less than 1 gram; Saturated Fat: 0.2 gram; Sodium: 114 milligrams; Cholesterol: 3 milligrams.

STRAWBERRY SMOOTHIE

Rookie

INGREDIENTS:

1 cup frozen strawberries, packed *without* syrup
½ teaspoon vanilla extract

1 cup nonfat or low-fat vanilla yogurt
1 cup ice cubes (optional)

DIRECTIONS:

1. Place the strawberries, vanilla, yogurt, and ice in a blender or food processor. Blend until the mixture looks frothy and the ice cubes have been crushed, about 4 minutes.

2. Stir with a wooden spoon to check that all of the strawberries and ice cubes are blended. Pour into tall glasses.

Per serving: Calories: 102; Total Fat: less than 1 gram; Saturated Fat: 0.1 gram; Sodium: 75 milligrams; Cholesterol: 3 milligrams.

BANANA SMOOTHIE

Intermediate

INGREDIENTS:

1 medium-size banana,
    about 6 inches long
1 cup skim milk

1 teaspoon vanilla extract
1 teaspoon honey
1 cup ice cubes (optional)

DIRECTIONS:

1. Peel the banana and cut into chunks.

2. Place the banana, milk, vanilla, honey, and ice in a blender or food processor. Blend until the mixture looks smooth, about 4 minutes.

3. Turn off the blender or processor. Stir with a wooden spoon to check that all of the ingredients are thoroughly mixed. Serve in tall glasses.

Per serving: Calories: 114; Total Fat: less than 1 gram; Saturated Fat: 0.3 gram; Sodium: 64 milligrams; Cholesterol: 2 milligrams.

APRICOT SMOOTHIE

Rookie

INGREDIENTS:

$3/4$ cup canned apricots,
    packed in water or
    light syrup
$1/2$ cup orange juice

$1/2$ cup nonfat or low-fat
    vanilla yogurt
$1 1/2$ cups ice cubes
    (optional)

DIRECTIONS:

1. Open the canned apricots and drain the liquid.

2. Place the apricots, orange juice, yogurt, and ice in a blender or processor and blend until smooth. Stir with a wooden spoon to check that all of the ingredients are thoroughly mixed. Serve in tall glasses.

Per serving: Calories: 116; Total Fat: less than 1 gram; Saturated Fat: 0.1 gram; Sodium: 42 milligrams; Cholesterol: 2 milligrams.

MELON SMOOTHIE

Rookie

INGREDIENTS:

1 cup frozen melon balls or cubes (cantaloupe or honeydew)
½ cup skim milk

½ cup nonfat or low-fat vanilla yogurt
1 cup ice cubes (optional)
Cinnamon

DIRECTIONS:

1. Blend the melon, milk, yogurt, and ice in a blender or food processor until smooth. Turn off the blender or processor and stir the smoothie with a wooden spoon to make sure that the melon is all blended.

2. Pour into tall glasses and top with a gentle shake of cinnamon.

Per serving: Calories: 97; Total Fat: less than 1 gram; Saturated Fat: 0.1 gram; Sodium: 95 milligrams; Cholesterol: 3 milligrams.

MIXED-FRUIT SMOOTHIE

Intermediate

INGREDIENTS:

1 medium-size peach (or
   1 can sliced peaches
   in juice or light
   syrup)
1 medium-size banana

1 cup nonfat or low-fat
   fruit-flavored
   (strawberry or
   blueberry) yogurt
1 cup ice cubes (optional)

DIRECTIONS:

1. Peel and slice the peach (or open the can and drain the liquid). Peel and slice the banana.

2. Place the peach slices, banana, yogurt, and ice in a blender or food processor and blend until smooth, about 3 minutes. Turn the blender or processor off. Stir with a wooden spoon to make sure the fruit is completely blended. Pour into tall glasses and serve.

Per serving: Calories: 160; Total Fat: less than 1 gram; Saturated Fat: 1 gram; Sodium: 41 milligrams; Cholesterol: 3 milligrams.

Note: Nutritional analyses for all smoothies are based on using low-fat yogurt.

INDEX